AMERICAN POETS PROJECT

IS PUBLISHED WITH A GIFT IN MEMORY OF

James Merrill

AND SUPPORT FROM ITS FOUNDING PATRONS

Sidney J. Weinberg, Jr. Foundation

The Berkley Foundation

Richard B. Fisher and Jeanne Donovan Fisher

John Greenleaf Whittier

selected poems

brenda wineapple editor

AMERICAN POETS PROJECT

THE LIBRARY OF AMERICA

The paper used in this publication meets the minimum requirements of the
American National Standard for Information Sciences—Permanence of Paper
for Printed Library Materials, ANSI Z39.48—1984.

Design by Chip Kidd and Mark Melnick.
Frontispiece: 1833 portrait of John Greenleaf Whittier by Deacon Robert
Peckham courtesy Special Collections, Haverhill Public Library, Haverhill,
MA, and the Trustees of the John Greenleaf Whittier Birthplace.

Library of Congress Cataloging-in-Publication Data:
Whittier John Greenleaf, 1807–1892.
   [Poems. Selections]
   Selected poems / John Greenleaf Whittier; Brenda Wineapple, editor.
      p. cm. — (American poets project ; 10)
      Includes bibliographical references and index.
      ISBN 1–931082–59–6 (alk. paper)
      I. Wineapple, Brenda. II. Title. III. Series.
 PS3252.W47 2004
 811'.3 — dc22
 2003060483

10 9 8 7 6 5 4 3 2 1

John
Greenleaf
Whittier

CONTENTS

INTRODUCTION

Once upon a time the poetry of John Greenleaf Whittier was force-fed to generations of schoolchildren, myself among them, who suffered, claustrophobic, through the masterpiece *Snow-Bound*, never for a moment understanding what we read. I was in the eighth grade, my family having recently returned to Haverhill, Massachusetts, Whittier's birthplace (and my mother's), and I shuffled off to school—the John Greenleaf Whittier school, of course —where in the first confusing days, I was temporarily placed in a class instructed by a Fireside Teacher whom I hated on first sight. Whittier didn't help. It all seemed so, well, *local*.

Disaffected, I longed for the alienation *Snow-Bound* can't provide. I did not know and was not told that the Quaker poet I resented actually put his life and his verse on the line, writing poetry committed to the abolition of slavery. At 12, I knew only *Snow-Bound* and could not care less about its "Flemish pictures of old days"; its gray-winged

"Angel of the backward look" seemed as beside the point as its unbroken surface. Later I realized I had been too young for the poem, and now I suspect that all the school-children subjected to Whittier's assurances are themselves too callow to understand, never mind care, how memory fends off the mindlessness of winter storm. After all, the highly descriptive and introspective *Snow-Bound* is not just about a moment of rural life, beautifully evoked and by-gone; it's a lyrical, lovely, and all-too-fragile hedge against the "coldness visible" that turns the world to white.

"Sit with me by the homestead hearth," invites the poet near *Snow-Bound*'s end,

> And stretch the hands of memory forth
>   To warm them at the wood-fire's blaze!
> And thanks untraced to lips unknown
> Shall greet me like the odors blown
> From unseen meadows newly mown,
> Or lilies floating in some pond,
> Wood-fringed, the wayside gaze beyond;
> The traveller owns the grateful sense
> Of sweetness near, he knows not whence,
> And, pausing, takes with forehead bare
> The benediction of the air.

At an early age, Whittier worked the farm and roamed the woods or climbed Job's Hill, which rose almost directly out of the family garden. In the house, there was a Bible but few other books, and the only annual was an almanac. Whittier later said that whenever he heard of a biography or volume of travel, he'd walk miles, doubtless through snow, to borrow it. But when William Lloyd Garrison began his weekly paper, the *Free Press*, in nearby Newbury-port, Whittier's father, impressed, canceled his subscription to the *Haverhill Gazette*.

Whittier is a poet of place, and his place is fundamentally New England, where generations of Whittiers, turned Quaker, had lived since the poet's great-great-grandfather Thomas came to America in 1638. Settling permanently in the village of Haverhill, he then built the old farmhouse in sight of no other home, just miles of woodland and, to the west, a pasture dotted with oaks and walnuts. The poet's father was a hardscrabble farmer, often in debt, and a town selectman with scant use for literature: "A prompt, decisive man, no breath / Our father wasted," Whittier would write of him in *Snow-Bound*.

Whittier's literary mentor was the schoolmaster, Joshua Coffin, who brought a volume of Robert Burns to the Whittier homestead to recite aloud. Whittier was mesmerized—and thrilled when Coffin loaned him the book. A sensitive child, the boy was already living a double life, hunting eggs hidden in the barn by day and secretly reading Walter Scott's *The Pirate* at night by candlelight while fantasizing about the adventures he early put into rhyme. In 1826, his elder sister Mary mailed one of her brother's poems to the *Free Press*; Garrison printed it and another one, then drove out to Haverhill to meet the 19-year-old contributor and urge his father to send the boy to school. "Sir, poetry will not get him bread," Whittier's father reportedly answered.

Unfazed, at least outwardly, Whittier learned how to sew ladies' slippers for eight cents a pair and pocketed enough money for a six-month stint at the Haverhill Academy. Unlike his peers Henry Wadsworth Longfellow or James Russell Lowell, he did not attend college or teach at Harvard and was not, as poet Richard Howard said of Longfellow, "fatally fluent." Whittier was, in essence, a poor farmer's son, a poor man, and an autodidact, insecure but without pretension. "I am not a builder in the sense of

Milton's phrase of one who could 'build the lofty rhyme,'"
he once said of his work. "My vehicles have been of the
humbler sort—merely the farm wagon and buckboard of
verse."

Yet verse was his life. Conscious of his meager educa-
tion and a modest man despite world-class ambitions, in-
versely proportional to his poverty, toward the end of his
life Whittier scrupulously told a biographer to anticipate
the criticism readers would no doubt continue heaping on
his work. "Touch upon my false rhymes and Yankeeisms,"
he instructed. "Own that I sometimes choose unpoetical
themes. Endorse Lowell's 'Fable for Critics,' that I mis-
take, occasionally, simple excitement for inspiration." For
Lowell, in his 1848 send-up of contemporary writers, had
echoed the popular view of Whittier:

Let his mind once get head in its favorite direction,
And the torrent of verse bursts the dams of reflection,
While, borne with the rush of the metre along,
The poet may chance to go right or go wrong,
Content with the whirl and delirium of song;
Then his grammar's not always correct, nor his rhymes,
And he's prone to repeat his own lyrics sometimes,—
Not his best, though, for those are struck off at
    white-heats,
When the heart in his breast like a trip-hammer beats.

To a well-heeled versifier like Lowell, Whittier was a
rustic. But Whittier was well-read and even fairly catholic
in his taste. He quoted Laurence Sterne almost obsessively,
loved the *Bhagavad-Gita*, Edmund Burke, Edmund Spenser,
Dante, Cervantes, Lamartine, Shelley, and Coleridge.
Among American authors he admired Lowell, Emerson,
Longfellow, Hawthorne, and Oliver Wendell Holmes. He
considered Poe an "extraordinary genius" but was less sure

of Thoreau, of whom he wrote: "Thoreau's 'Walden' is capital reading but very wicked and heathenish. The practical moral of it seems to be that if a man is willing to sink himself into a woodchuck, he can live as cheaply as that quadruped; but after all, for me I prefer walking on two legs." Not surprisingly, he didn't know Dickinson, and he regarded Walt Whitman as a "tender" man who, alas, rode an "untamed, rough-jolting Pegasus." When asked to help purchase a horse and buggy for Whitman, then partially paralyzed, Whittier sent ten dollars though he fretted lest the public might think he endorsed the "sensual school" of literature.

Whitman acknowledged that he and Whittier "would not travel well harnessed to the same rig," but he recognized and respected Whittier's "out-cropping love of heroism and war, for all his Quakerdom[;] his verses at times [are] like the measur'd step of Cromwell's old veterans." Whittier understood this side of himself but thought that "Few guessed beneath his aspect grave/What passions strove in chains." Whitman wasn't the only one who sensed the fire sizzling under Quaker drab. A friend, Edna Dean Proctor, observed, "I have always been impressed by the mingled volcano and iceberg of your character."

Despite flirtations with various women, Whittier never married. Tall, dark, and good-looking, since youth he complained of an array of ailments: palpitations, headaches, neuralgia, eyestrain, back pain, and insomnia, maladies that released him, over time, from farm chores, unwanted visitors, solicitations, speaking engagements, and commitment. "I always did love a pretty girl," he wrote as if in retrospect at the age of 22, adding "the worst of it is— if I ever get married I must marry a Quakeress with her bonnet like a flour dipper, and a face as long as a tobacco yawl." Loyal to the religion of his birth, he was suggesting that it, along with his sundry complaints, stood between himself and marriage. Later he admitted to a friend, "I think I have left a great many roses in my life for fear of the thorns."

Emotionally, he had long been sustained by his mother, Abigail Hussey Whittier, whom the poet remembered as speaking "The common unrhymed poetry/Of simple life and country ways." And he remained devoted to his unmarried sister Elizabeth, with whom he lived until her death, seeming more comfortable with her and the long-term friendships, particularly with women, that didn't threaten his bachelorhood or meddle with his work. Yet he was generous and supportive to writers like Lucy Larcom, Celia Thaxter, and Sarah Orne Jewett, whom he considered an adopted daughter; he exchanged witticisms with the acerbic Gail Hamilton; and after the death of his beloved editor James T. Fields, who first published his non-abolitionist poetry, Whittier grew closer to Fields' wife, Annie. Today, little evidence links Whittier with much of an erotic attachment to woman or to man—despite a smart-alecky interpretation of his "barefoot boy, with cheek of tan!"—though he did develop close friendships with men such as William Lloyd Garrison, for a time, and Charles Sumner.

Above all, Whittier was ambitious. "I am not one to be easily turned aside from any undertaking," he told a friend in youth, and to another, after reading a biography of Byron, he vowed: "I would not depart from this sphere of trial without leaving behind me a name to be remembered when I am dust." His preoccupation with fame persisted, though it was shaken by the poor reception given his first book of prose and verse, *Legends of New England*, published in 1831 when he was 23. He subsequently tried to destroy all copies of the book, and salvaged his pride by announcing: "The world shall know me in a loftier capacity than as a writer of rhymes."

When not working the farm or composing verse, Whittier earned an income as an editor, first of the *American Manufacturer* in Boston (a position he had secured through Garrison), then of the *Haverhill Gazette*, and later of the *New England Weekly Review* in Hartford, Connecticut. As editor, he was consistently active in politics, supporting Henry Clay's bid for the presidency and throwing his increasing weight around in local elections. "Politics is the only field now open for me," he told the poet Lydia Sigourney. "The truth is, I don't care a fig for poetical reputation," he wrote to another friend, "and I had much rather be known as an ardent friend of republican principles." Of course, he was posturing. Whittier had no intention of giving up poetry but needed to square it with his Quaker conscience and a more sober assessment of his talent. Shaking off the influence of Burns, he began to write, without conflict, of the political issues near his heart. As he subsequently explained, he

> with a mission to fulfil
> Had left the Muses' haunts to turn
> The crank of an opinion-mill,
> Making his rustic reed of song
> A Weapon in the war with wrong.

"Although I am a Quaker by birthright and sincere convictions," he once said, "I am no sectarian in the strict sense of the term. My sympathies are with the Broad Church of Humanity." As a Quaker, Whittier had been educated to consider slavery the scourge of the country, and as early as 1833 he joined forces with the nascent anti-slavery movement spearheaded by Garrison (with whom he later broke rank). Whittier printed at his own expense the pamphlet *Justice and Expediency; or, Slavery considered with a view to its Rightful and Effectual Remedy, Abolition* (1833), and filled newspapers with a tough-fibered prose, pushing for complete emancipation and the eradication of all prejudice based on skin color. "The tremendous sin of our country, which lies at the bottom of Slavery," he wrote in 1835, was "Hatred of the Black Man." Again, seven years later: "I hate slavery in all its forms, degrees and influences," Whittier declared, "and I deem myself bound by the highest moral and political obligations not to let that sentiment of hate lie dormant and smouldering in my own breast, but to give it free vent and let it blaze forth, that it may kindle equal ardor through the whole sphere of my influence."

Attending the first national anti-slavery convention in Philadelphia and drafting its Declaration of Sentiments, Whittier had also been a delegate to the national Republican convention and a candidate for the Massachusetts legislature, though he was disqualified because of his young age: he was just short of 26. But he was, even then, a crack political operator who, if not exactly in the fray, pulled the levers behind the scenes. For many years, he held Massachusetts congressman Caleb Cushing's toes to the abolitionist fire; he conspired with John Quincy Adams, and believing that the cause would be served best by practical politics, he helped found the Liberty party, a precursor to the new Republican party, running for Congress on its anti-slavery ticket. In 1864, he was instrumental in convincing John C. Frémont not to split the party by opposing Lincoln.

For his pains, a mob in Concord, New Hampshire, pelted the Quaker abolitionist with stones and mud when he accompanied the British anti-slavery activist George Thompson on a lecture tour, and on another occasion he was battered by rotten eggs and sticks in Newburyport. (Hawthorne, a staunch anti-abolitionist, gently poked fun at Whittier, whom he characterized fancifully as "a fiery Quaker youth, to whom the muse had perversely assigned a battle-trumpet, and who got himself lynched, ten years ago, in South Carolina.") In the spring of 1838 when he was editor of *The Pennsylvania Freeman*, a paper of the Anti-Slavery Society, an angry rabble sacked his office in the basement of Pennsylvania Hall, which was burned beyond recognition as the crowd shouted "hang Whittier." The poet barely escaped with his life.

Among his earliest anti-slavery poems was "Touissaint l'Ouverture" (1833), about the 1794 slave uprising in Haiti which includes an account of the rape of a French planter's wife so brutal that the literary historian Perry Miller commented it was probably one of the least useful contributions to the abolitionist cause since it could be construed as an argument against, not for, emancipation. If the poem doesn't entirely succeed—despite stirring scenes, it's somewhat diffuse—we need to remember that to Whittier poems are not well-wrought urns. They were meant to be read, sung, shouted, or printed on broadsides, and they took their structure from ballads, hymns, slogans, folk tales, sermons, and vernacular speech. During the Civil War, when the Hutchinson family sang Whittier's ballad "Ein feste Burg ist unser Gott," based on Luther's hymn, it created such a fuss that General McClellan forbade the family to sing it to the troops—until, that is, Lincoln heard the song and renewed the permit.

Whittier did not think his readers would always agree with him—they decidedly didn't—but he wanted to stir their emotions, raise their dander, let them know how he felt. He intended to inspire, not to belittle, and in the matter of abolition he aimed literally to create an audience.

(One could say he was eventually successful.) His moral compass clear, his sensibility proudly undissociated, Whittier did not evade, sidestep, or vamp about his convictions. He used no self-irony. His satires were direct, his forms conventional, his narratives linear, his hand open. Angry and at times doubtful ("How little, after all do we *know*?"), he offered readers not just the consolations of form but of belief. "What I had I gave," he writes in his long anti-slavery poem "The Panorama." He is no Prufrock.

In much of his verse, he could wield a language of forceful immediacy—the "blood-red sky" of "Toussaint l'Ouverture"—or make his rhythms pliant, as in "The Farewell," where the Virginia slave mother cries, over and over, "Gone, gone—sold and gone." In "The Hunters of Men," the ballad form and galloping rhythm work well to deride with grim humor anyone, white or black, female or male, cleric or banker, who collaborates in human debasement:

> So speed to their hunting, o'er mountain and glen,
> Through cane-brake and forest,— the hunting of men!

In "Song of Slaves in the Desert," Whittier dramatizes the awestruck cry of a dispossessed people, who ask in refrain, "Where are we going, Rubee?" as the poem's five stanzas take them progressively farther from home. That they never relinquish hope, in their despair, renders the poem supple and heart-piercing.

> When we went from Bornou land,
> We were like the leaves and sand,—
> We were many, we are few;
> Life has one, and death has two:
> Whitened bones our path are showing,
> Thou All-seeing, thou All-knowing!

Hear us, tell us, where are we going,
Where are we going, Rubee?

Whittier clearly felt that poetry could be—although did not have to be—socially engaged, but he never believed poetry should subordinate itself to political necessity or rank didacticism. "There is something inconsistent in the character of a poet & a modern politician," he remarked as early as 1832 as he set out to bring the two worlds together. But by 1840, the abolitionist poet was himself testy on the subject of abolitionist verse. "The thing is getting to be sadly over done," Whittier groused. "Everybody rhymes for them—as if an abolitionist must be ex-officio a rhymer, as one of the Shaking Fraternity must be a dancer,—a sort of philanthropic Della Cruscan Style in which 'slavery's night' jingles with 'Truth and Right'— and 'down-trodden slave' treads upon 'Freedom's grave.'"

A self-critical man to whom versifying came naturally, and sometimes too easily, Whittier valued a poetry, whether political or not, of imagination. He excelled at dramatic monologues, similar in genre to Browning's although different in purpose, and showed real fluidity in this line in his only novel—a good one—called *Leaves from Margaret Smith's Journal*, in which he impersonates a young English woman visiting Massachusetts Bay in 1678. Here, and in principle, Whittier knew the difference between resistance and harangue, faith and dry dogma. His chief gripe against Transcendentalist verse, for example, was that "its largest intent is ethical and religious and not artistic."

If the charge that he is overly didactic or merely topical is to be flung against Whittier, it doesn't stick to a rhetorically powerful, intricately allusive poem like "Ichabod!" in which he expresses his disillusionment with the once-mighty orator Daniel Webster. Webster had supported the Compromise of 1850 with its nefarious Fugitive Slave Bill (proposed by another of Whittier's former idols, Henry Clay), allowing slave owners to enter free states, seize runaway slaves—kidnap them, according to the abolitionists—and drag them back to the South. Whittier's response was a kind of eulogy, its anger muted into condescension:

> When faith is lost, when honor dies
> The man is dead!

Less complex lyrics, like "A Sabbath Scene," are also affecting, as are satires like the "Letter . . . from a Missionary of the Methodist Episcopal Church," with its offhand horrors made conversational. "Here, at the Mission, all things have gone well," writes the missionary,

> The brother who, throughout my absence, acted
> As overseer, assures me that the crops
> Never were better. I have lost one negro,
> A first-rate hand, but obstinate and sullen.
> He ran away some time last spring, and hid
> In the river timber. There my Indian converts
> Found him, and treed and shot him. For the rest,
> The heathens round about begin to feel
> The influence of our pious ministrations
> And works of love; and some of them already
> Have purchased negroes, and are settling down
> As sober Christians! Bless the Lord for this!

We did not read these poems, or "The Haschish," in school.

True, not all of Whittier's work succeeds in showing off his imagination. At times he seems almost afraid of it, as if it really were that fat wheezing demon of his study, the subject of one of his earliest poems. Yet had we, years ago, read his poems about slavery, war, injustice, or any of his comic ballads and dramatic monologues, we wouldn't have run so fast from what appeared as—and could be—pat moralization or facile optimism. We may even have discovered that the easily parodied "Maud Muller" is shrewder than we thought, "Telling the Bees" more adroit, and Whittier's verse forms, overall, more varied. But my generation (the last, no doubt, to read Whittier under duress) assigned him to the backroom of literature, and we missed the jarring images—"white pagodas of the snow" or "moony breadth of virgin face, / By thought unviolated"— as well as the tender plea in a touching poem like "The Eternal Goodness":

> And Thou, O Lord! by whom are seen
>   Thy creatures as they be,
> Forgive me if too close I lean
>   My human heart on Thee!

Whittier often wrote better, more courageously, and with more beauty than we knew.

Consider too the poems where despair almost shatters nature's benign casing. With simple grace, he describes outward circumstance and inner feeling, often both in the same poem. "The Garrison at Cape Ann," for instance, begins as a reminiscence of his walking along the "breezy headlands" on a summer morning; it proceeds to finely etch the garrison house, near the "rude and broken coastline, white with breakers stretching north,—" and its occupants, those soldiers who amuse themselves through the night telling stories until, by spectral sounds, they load their muskets and fire into nothingness. Whittier concludes, in the penultimate stanza, that

Soon or late to all our dwellings come the spectres of the
     mind,
Doubts and fears and dread forebodings, in the darkness
     undefined;
Round us throng the grim projections of the heart and of
     the brain,
And our pride of strength is weakness, and the cunning
     hand is vain.

This is a poet who knows of desert spaces.

"The loneliness of life, under even its best circum-
stances, becomes, at times, appalling to contemplate,"
Whittier told a friend. "No one human soul ever fully
knew another; and an infinite sigh for sympathy is perpet-
ually going up from the heart of humanity." But, like
Emerson—or Wallace Stevens—Whittier has a knack for
recovery. "Doubtless this very unrest and longing is the
prophecy and guaranty of an immortal destination," he
continued. "Perfect content is stagnation and ultimate
death."

After the Civil War, Whittier increasingly wrote con-
trolled poems of a reflective cast culminating in *Snow-
Bound*, which was prompted in part by the deaths of Whit-
tier's mother in 1857 and of his beloved sister Elizabeth in
1864. Selling 20,000 copies in the first months of its publi-
cation, *Snow-Bound* rocketed the poet to fame. Reputedly,
the poem's staggering success had to do with America's de-
sire to flee a complicated present in the aftermath of war,
taking refuge in a child's world of blithe ignorance and
family value.   But this reading violates the spirit of the
poem. Not only does Whittier keep beating the drum of
reform, the poem is less a work of escapism than a medita-
tion on the inevitable "loss in all familiar things."

> The sun that brief December day
> Rose cheerless over hills of gray, . . .

Whittier writes of the inexorability of the winter season when snow falls fast, its white drifts resembling "tall and sheeted ghosts." The air turns savage, the winds shriek, and one little group—one among many—huddles indoors to stave off its terror with stories. Much as the poet does: he too, his own "hair as gray / As was my sire's that winter day," takes comfort, small as it is, in the mind that replenishes by recreating. Such is the benediction, to him, of poetry: it transforms sorrow and affliction into words that are poised, straightforward and, in their unvarnished way, brave.

The somewhat romanticized portrait of rural life in *Snow-Bound* was followed by the "Prelude" to *Among the Hills* (1869), a poem that reveals Whittier at his scrupulous best. Here he also presents in plain and speechlike language, startling in its directness, and without a trace of idealization, the rural world he knew well:

> Within, the cluttered kitchen-floor, unwashed
> (Broom-clean I think they called it); the best room
> Stifling with cellar damp, shut from the air
> In hot midsummer, bookless, pictureless
> Save the inevitable sampler hung
> Over the fireplace, or a mourning-piece,
> A green-haired woman, peony-cheeked, beneath
> Impossible willows. . . .

Whittier was by now something of a public treasure, with his birthdays celebrated nationally, and more than a hundred hymns extracted from his poems. (The most renowned of these was the last section, "Dear Lord and Father of mankind," in the otherwise somewhat incongruous poem, "The Brewing of Soma.") He continued to be politically active, backing local office-seekers, advocating full civil rights for all citizens, supporting woman suffrage, and protesting both the avarice of the carpetbaggers and the atrocities of the Ku Klux Klan.

His private life remained as sequestered as ever, and he continued to plead poor health as a way of protecting himself from the unsought requests of well-wishers and fans. Now, though, his symptoms spelled mortality, and with death stalking his friends from abolitionist days—Horace Greeley, Charles Sumner, and then Garrison in 1879—Whittier grew more and more troubled. His literary world began to disappear: Fields died and then Emerson and Longfellow, leaving Whittier to remark to Oliver Wendell Holmes that "we seem to hear our roots cracking."

Chills, fever, and insomnia notwithstanding, Whittier continued to publish volumes of verse prolifically, issuing nine collections between 1870 and 1886. His last book, the privately printed *At Sundown*, appeared posthumously in 1892, and contained one of the last poems he wrote, "To Oliver Wendell Holmes." The terms in which he addresses his longtime friend might well serve to introduce the old poet to a new reader:

> Life is indeed no holiday; therein
>   Are want, and woe, and sin,
> Death and its nameless fears, and over all
>   Our pitying tears must fall.
>
> Sorrow is real; but the counterfeit
>   Which folly brings to it,
> We need thy wit and wisdom to resist,
>   O rarest Optimist!

> Thy hand, old friend! the service of our days,
>   In differing moods and ways,
> May prove to those who follow in our train
>   Not valueless nor vain.

Revisited now, Whittier appears fresh, honest, even flinty and practical. His diction is easy, his detail rich and unassuming, his emotion deep. And the shale of his New England landscape reaches outward, promising not relief from pain but a glimpse of a better, larger world.

One more thing: Whitman also took another look. For Whittier's 80th birthday, December 17, 1887, the good gray poet, large and wise, celebrated a fellow traveler:

> As the Greek's signal flame, by antique records told,
> Rose from the hill-top, like applause and glory,
> Welcoming in fame some special veteran, hero,
> With rosy tinge reddening the land he'd served,
> So I aloft from Mannahatta's ship-fringed shore,
> Lift high a kindled brand for thee, Old Poet.

Brenda Wineapple
2003

Toussaint l'Ouverture

The moon was up. One general smile
Was resting on the Indian isle—
Mild—pure—ethereal; rock and wood,
In searching sunshine, wild and rude,
Rose, mellowed through the silver gleam,
Soft as the landscape of a dream:
All motionless and dewy wet,
Tree, vine, and flower in shadow met:
The myrtle with its snowy bloom,
Crossing the nightshade's solemn gloom—
The white cecropia's silver rhind
Relieved by deeper green behind—
The orange with its fruit of gold,—
The lithe paullinia's verdant fold,—
The passion-flower with symbol holy,
Twining its tendrils long and lowly,—
The rhexias dark, and cassia tall,
And, proudly rising over all,
The kingly palm's imperial stem,
Crowned with its leafy diadem,—
Star-like, beneath whose sombre shade,
The fiery-winged cucullo played!

Yes—lovely was thine aspect, then,
   Fair island of the Western Sea!—
Lavish of beauty, even when
Thy brutes were happier than thy men,

For *they*, at least, were *free*!
Regardless of thy glorious clime,
   Unmindful of thy soil of flowers,
The toiling negro sighed, that Time
   No faster sped his hours.
For, by the dewy moonlight still,
He fed the weary-turning mill,
Or bent him in the chill morass,
To pluck the long and tangled grass,
And hear above his scar-worn back
The heavy slave-whip's frequent crack;—
While in his heart one evil thought
In solitary madness wrought,—
One baleful fire surviving still,
   The quenching of th'immortal mind—
   One sterner passion of his kind,
Which even fetters could not kill,—
The savage hope, to deal, ere long,
A vengeance bitterer than his wrong!

Hark to that cry!—long, loud, and shrill,
From field and forest, rock and hill,
Thrilling and horrible it rung,
   Around, beneath, above;—
The wild beast from his cavern sprung—
   The wild bird from her grove!
Nor fear, nor joy, nor agony
Were mingled in that midnight cry;
But, like the lion's growl of wrath,
When falls that hunter in his path

Whose barbed arrow, deeply set,
Is rankling in his bosom yet,
It told of hate, full, deep and strong,—
Of vengeance kindling out of wrong;
It was as if the crimes of years—
The agony—the toil—the tears—
The shame and hate, which liken well
Earth's garden to the nether hell,
Had found in Nature's self a tongue,
On which the gathered horror hung;
As if from cliff, and stream, and glen,
Burst, on the startled ears of men,
That voice which rises unto God—
Solemn and stern—the cry of blood!

It ceased—and all was still once more,
Save ocean chafing on his shore—
The sighing of the wind between
The broad banana's leaves of green—
Or, bough by restless plumage shook—
Or, distant brawl of mountain brook.

Brief was the silence. Once again
    Pealed to the skies that frantic yell—
Glowed on the heavens a fiery stain,
    And flashes rose and fell;
And, painted on the blood-red sky,
Dark, naked arms were tossed on high;
And, round the white man's lordly hall,
    Trod, fierce and free, *the brute he made*;

And those who crept along the wall,
And answered to his lightest call
   With more than spaniel dread.
The creatures of his lawless beck
Were trampling on his very neck!
And, on the night-air, wild and clear,
Rose woman's shriek of more than fear;
For bloodied arms were round her thrown,
And dark cheeks pressed against her own!

Then, injured Afric, for the shame
Of thy own daughters, vengeance came
Full on the scornful hearts of those,
Who mocked thee in thy nameless woes,
And to thy hapless children gave
One choice—pollution, or the grave!

Dark-browed Toussaint!—the storm had risen
   Obedient to his master-call—
The Negro's mind had burst its prison—
   His hand its iron thrall!
Yet where was he, whose fiery zeal
First taught the trampled heart to feel,
Until despair itself grew strong,
And vengeance fed its torch from wrong?
Now—when the thunder-bolt is speeding—
Now—when oppression's heart is bleeding—
Now—when the latent curse of Time
   Is raining down in fire and blood—
That curse, which through long years of crime,
   Had gathered, drop by drop, its flood:

Why strikes he not, the foremost one,
Where Murder's sternest deeds are done?

He stood the aged palms beneath,
   That shadowed o'er his humble door,
Listening, with half-suspended breath,
To the wild sounds of fear and death,
   —Toussaint l'Ouverture!
What marvel that his heart beat high!
   The blow for freedom had been given;
And blood had answered to the cry
   Which earth sent up to heaven!
What marvel, that a fierce delight
Smiled grimly o'er his brow of night,
As groan, and shout, and bursting flame,
Told where the midnight tempest came;
With blood and fire along its van,
And death behind!—he was a MAN!

Yes,—dark-souled chieftain!—if the light
   Of mild Religion's heavenly ray
Unveiled not to thy mental sight
   The lowlier and the purer way,
In which the Holy Sufferer trod,
   Meekly amidst the sons of crime,—
That calm reliance upon God
   For justice, in his own good time,—
That gentleness, to which belongs
Forgiveness for its many wrongs;
Even as the primal martyr, kneeling
For mercy on the evil-dealing,—

Let not the favored white man name
Thy stern appeal, with words of blame.
Has *he* not, with the light of heaven
    Broadly around him, made the same—
Yea,—on a thousand war-fields striven,
    And gloried in his open shame?
Kneeling amidst his brothers' blood,
To offer mockery unto God,
As if the High and Holy One
Could smile on deeds of murder done!—
As if a human sacrifice
Were purer in   His holy eyes,
Though offered up by Christian hands,
Than the foul rites of Pagan lands!

.   .   .   .   .

Sternly, amidst his household band,
His carbine grasped within his hand,
    The white man stood, prepared and still,
Waiting the shock of maddened men,
Unchained, and fierce as tigers, when
    The horn winds through their caverned hill.
And one was weeping in his sight,
    The fairest flower of all the isle,—
The bride who seemed but yesternight
    The image of a smile.
And, clinging to her trembling knee,
Looked up the form of infancy,
With tearful glance in either face,
The secret of its fear to trace.

'Ha—stand, or die!' The white man's eye
    His steady musket gleamed along,
As a tall Negro hastened nigh,
    With fearless step and strong.
'What ho, Toussaint!' A moment more,
His shadow crossed the lighted floor.
'Away!' he shouted; 'fly with me,—
The white man's bark is on the sea;—
Her sails must catch the landward wind,
For sudden vengeance sweeps behind.
Our brethren from their graves have spoken,
The yoke is spurned—the chain is broken;
On all the hills our fires are glowing—
Through all the vales red blood is flowing!
No more the mocking White shall rest
His foot upon the Negro's breast;—
No more, at morn or eve, shall drip
The warm blood from the driver's whip:—
Yet, though Toussaint has vengeance sworn
For all the wrongs his race have borne,—
Though for each drop of Negro blood,
The white man's veins shall pour a flood;
Not all alone the sense of ill
Around his heart is lingering still,
Nor deeper can the white man feel
The generous warmth of grateful zeal.
Friends of the Negro! fly with me—
The path is open to the sea:
Away, for life!'—He spoke, and pressed
The young child to his manly breast,
As, headlong, through the cracking cane,

Down swept the dark insurgent train—
Drunken and grim—with shout and yell
Howled through the dark, like sounds from hell!

Far out, in peace, the white man's sail
Swayed free before the sunrise gale.
Cloud-like that island hung afar,
   Along the bright horizon's verge,
O'er which the curse of servile war
   Rolled its red torrent, surge on surge.
And he—the Negro champion,—where
   In the fierce tumult, struggled he?
Go trace him by the fiery glare
Of dwellings in the midnight air—
The yells of triumph and despair—
   The streams that crimson to the sea!

Sleep calmly in thy dungeon-tomb,
   Beneath Besancon's alien sky,
Dark Haytian!—for the time shall come,—
   Yea, even now is nigh—
When, every where, thy name shall be
Redeemed from *color's infamy*;
And men shall learn to speak of thee,
As one of earth's great spirits, born
In servitude, and nursed in scorn,
Casting aside the weary weight
And fetters of its low estate,
In that strong majesty of soul,
   Which knows no color, tongue or clime—

Which still hath spurned the base control
    Of tyrants through all time!
For other hands than mine may wreath
The laurel round thy brow of death,
And speak thy praise, as one whose word
A thousand fiery spirits stirred,—
Who crushed his foeman as a worm—
Whose step on human hearts fell firm:—
Be mine the better task to find
A tribute for thy lofty mind,
Amidst whose gloomy vengeance shone
Some milder virtues all thine own,—
Some gleams of feeling pure and warm,
Like sunshine on a sky of storm,—
Proofs that the Negro's heart retains
Some nobleness amid its chains,—
That kindness to the wronged is never
    Without its excellent reward,—
Holy to human-kind, and ever,
    Acceptable to God.

The Demon of the Study

The Brownie sits in the Scotchman's room,
    And eats his meat and drinks his ale,
And beats the maid with her unused broom,
    And the lazy lout with his idle flail,
But he sweeps the floor and threshes the corn,
And hies him away ere the break of dawn.

The shade of Denmark fled from the sun,
    And the Cocklane ghost from the barn loft cheer,
The fiend of Faust was a faithful one,
    Agrippa's demon wrought in fear,
And the devil of Martin Luther sat
By the stout Monk's side in social chat.

The Old Man of the Sea, on the neck of him
    Who seven times crossed the deep,
Twined closely each lean and withered limb,
    Like the night-mare in one's sleep.
But he drank of the wine, and Sinbad cast
The evil weight from his back at last.

But the demon that cometh day by day
    To my quiet room and fire-side nook,
Where the casement light falls dim and gray
    On faded painting and ancient book,
Is a sorrier one than any whose names
Are chronicled well by good king James.

No bearer of burdens like Caliban,
    No runner of errands like Ariel,
He comes in the shape of a fat old man,
    Without rap of knuckle or pull of bell:
And whence he comes, or whither he goes,
I know as I do of the wind which blows.

A stout old man with a greasy hat
    Slouched heavily down to his dark, red nose,
And two grey eyes enveloped in fat,

Looking through glasses with iron bows.
Read ye, and heed ye, and ye who can,
Guard well your doors from that fat old man!

He comes with a careless "how d'ye do,"
   And seats himself in my elbow chair;
And my morning paper and pamphlet new
   Fall forthwith under his special care,
And he wipes his glasses and clears his throat,
And, button by button, unfolds his coat.

And then he reads from paper and book,
   In a low and husky asthmatic tone,
With the stolid sameness of posture and look
   Of one who reads to himself alone;
And hour after hour on my senses come
That husky wheeze and that dolorous hum.

The price of stocks, the auction sales,
   The poet's song and the lover's glee,
The horrible murders, the seaboard gales,
   The marriage list and the *jeu d'esprit*,
All reach my ear in the self-same tone,—
I shudder at each, but the fiend reads on!

Oh! sweet as the lapse of water at noon
   O'er the mossy roots of some forest tree,
The sigh of the wind in the woods of June,
   Or sound of flutes o'er a moonlight sea,
Or the low soft music, perchance which seems
To float through the slumbering singer's dreams.

So sweet, so dear is the silvery tone,
    Of her in whose features I sometimes look,
As I sit at eve by her side alone,
    And we read by turns from the self-same book,
Some tale perhaps of the olden time,
Some lover's romance or quaint old rhyme.

Then when the story is one of woe,—
    Some prisoner's plaint through his dungeon-bar,
Her blue eye glistens with tears, and low
    Her voice sinks down like a moan afar;
And I seem to hear that prisoner's wail,
And his face looks on me worn and pale.

And when she reads some merrier song,
    Her voice is glad as an April bird's,
And when the tale is of war and wrong,
    A trumpet's summons is in her words,
And the rush of the hosts I seem to hear,
And see the tossing of plume and spear!

Oh, pity me then when, day by day,
    The stout fiend darkens my parlor door;
And reads me perchance the self-same lay
    Which melted in music the night before,
From lips as the lips of Hylas sweet,
And moved like twin roses which zephyrs meet!

I cross my floor with a nervous tread,
    I whistle and laugh and sing and shout,
I flourish my cane above his head,

And stir up the fire to roast him out;
I topple the chairs, and drum on the pane,
And press my hands on my ears, in vain!

I've studied Glanville and James the wise,
   And wizard black-letter tomes which treat
Of demons of every name and size,
   Which a Christian man is presumed to meet,
But never a hint and never a line
Can I find of a reading fiend like mine.

I've crossed the Psalter with Brady and Tate,
   And laid the Primer above them all,
I've nailed a horse shoe over the grate,
   And hung a wig to my parlor wall
One worn by a learned Judge they say
At Salem court in the witchcraft day!

"Conjuro te, sceleratissime,
   Abire ad tuum locum!"—still
Like a visible night-mare he sits by me—
   The exorcism has lost its skill;
And I hear again in my haunted room
The husky wheeze and the dolorous hum!

Ah!— commend me to Mary Magdalen
   With her seven-fold plagues—to the wandering Jew,
To the terrors which haunted Orestes when
   The furies his midnight curtains drew.
But charm him off, ye who charm him can,
That reading demon, that fat old man!—

The Hunters of Men

Have ye heard of our hunting, o'er mountain and glen
Through cane-brake and forest—the hunting of men?
The lords of our land to this hunting have gone,
As the fox-hunter follows the sound of the horn:
Hark—the cheer and the hallo! the crack of the whip,
And the yell of the hound as he fastens his grip!
All blithe are our hunters, and noble their match—
Though *hundreds* are caught, there are *millions* to catch:
So speed to their hunting, o'er mountain and glen,
Through cane-brake and forest—the hunting of men!

Gay luck to our hunters!—how nobly they ride
In the glow of their zeal, and the strength of their
       pride!—
The Priest with his cassock flung back on the wind,
Just screening the politic Statesman behind—
The saint and the sinner, with cursing and prayer—
The drunk and the sober, ride merrily there.
And woman,—kind woman—wife, widow and maid—
For *the good of the hunted*—is lending her aid:
Her foot's in the stirrup—her hand on the rein—
How blithely she rides to the hunting of men!

Oh! goodly and grand is our hunting to see,
In this 'land of the brave and this home of the free.'
Priest, warrior, and statesman, from Georgia to Maine,
All mounting the saddle—all grasping the rein—
Right merrily hunting the black man, whose sin
Is the curl of his hair and the hue of his skin!

Wo, now to the hunted who turns him at bay!
Will our hunters be turned from their purpose and prey?
Will their hearts fail within them?—their nerves
      tremble, when
All roughly they ride to the hunting of men?

Ho—ALMS for our hunters! all weary and faint
Wax the curse of the sinner and prayer of the saint.
The horn is wound faintly—the echoes are still
Over cane-brake and river, and forest and hill.
Haste—alms for our hunters! the hunted once more
Have turned from their flight with their backs to the
      shore:
What right have *they* here in the home of the white,
Shadowed o'er by *our* banner of Freedom and Right?
Ho—alms for the hunters! or never again
Will they ride in their pomp to the hunting of men!

ALMS—ALMS for our hunters! why *will* ye delay,
When their pride and their glory are melting away?
The parson has turned; for, on charge of his own,
Who goeth a warfare, or hunting, alone?
The politic statesman looks back with a sigh—
There is doubt in his heart there is fear in his eye.
Oh! haste, lest that doubting and fear shall prevail,
And the head of his steed take the place of his tail.
Oh! haste, ere he leave us! for who will ride then,
For pleasure or gain, to the hunting of men!

The Farewell

Of a Virginia slave mother to her daughters, sold into southern bondage

Gone, gone—sold and gone,
To the rice-swamp dank and lone,
Where the slave-whip ceaseless swings,
Where the noisome insect stings,
Where the Fever Demon strews
Poison with the falling dews,
Where the sickly sunbeams glare
Through the hot and misty air,—
Gone, gone—sold and gone,
To the rice-swamp dank and lone,
From Virginia's hills and waters,—
Woe is me, my stolen daughters!

Gone, gone—sold and gone,
To the rice-swamp dank and lone.
There no mother's eye is near them,
There no mother's ear can hear them;
Never, when the torturing lash
Seams their back with many a gash,
Shall a mother's kindness bless them,
Or a mother's arms caress them.
Gone, gone—sold and gone,
To the rice-swamp dank and lone,
From Virginia's hills and waters,—
Woe is me, my stolen daughters!

Gone, gone—sold and gone,
To the rice-swamp dank and lone.

Oh, when weary, sad, and slow,
From the fields at night they go,
Faint with toil, and rack'd with pain,
To their cheerless homes again—
There no brother's voice shall greet them—
There no father's welcome meet them.

     Gone, gone—sold and gone,
     To the rice-swamp dank and lone,
     From Virginia's hills and waters,—
     Woe is me, my stolen daughters!

     Gone, gone—sold and gone,
     To the rice-swamp dank and lone,
From the tree whose shadow lay
On their childhood's place of play—
From the cool spring where they drank—
Rock, and hill, and rivulet bank—
From the solemn house of prayer,
And the holy counsels there—

     Gone, gone—sold and gone,
     To the rice-swamp dank and lone,
     From Virginia's hills and waters,—
     Woe is me, my stolen daughters!

     Gone, gone—sold and gone,
     To the rice-swamp dank and lone—
Toiling through the weary day,
And at night the Spoiler's prey.
Oh, that they had earlier died,
Sleeping calmly, side by side,
Where the tyrant's power is o'er,

And the fetter galls no more!
        Gone, gone—sold and gone,
        To the rice-swamp dank and lone,
        From Virginia's hills and waters,—
        Woe is me, my stolen daughters!

        Gone, gone—sold and gone,
        To the rice-swamp dank and lone.
By the holy love He beareth—
By the bruised reed He spareth;
Oh, may He, to whom alone
All their cruel wrongs are known,
Still their hope and refuge prove,
With a more than mother's love.
        Gone, gone—sold and gone,
        To the rice-swamp dank and lone.
        From Virginia's hills and waters,—
        Woe is me, my stolen daughters!

Massachusetts to Virginia

The blast from Freedom's northern hills, upon its
        Southern way,
Bears greeting to Virginia, from Massachusetts Bay:—
No word of haughty challenging, nor battle-bugle's peal,
Nor steady tread of marching files, nor clang of
        horsemen's steel.

No trains of deep-mouthed cannon along our highways
       go—
Around our silent arsenals untrodden lies the snow;
And to the land-breeze of our ports, upon their errands
       far,
A thousand sails of Commerce swell, but none are
       spread for War.

We hear thy threats, Virginia! thy stormy words and
       high,
Swell harshly on the Southern winds which melt along
       our sky;
Yet, not one brown, hard hand foregoes its honest labor
       here;
No hewer of our mountain oaks suspends his axe in fear.

Wild are the waves which lash the reefs along St.
       George's bank;
Cold on the shore of Labrador the fog lies white and
       dank;
Through storm, and wave, and blinding mist, stout are
       the hearts which man
The fishing-smacks of Marblehead, the sea-boats of
       Cape Ann.

The cold North light, and wintry sun glare on their icy
       forms,
Bent grimly o'er their straining lines or wrestling with
       the storms;

Free as the winds they drive before, rough as the waves
    they roam,
They laugh to scorn the slaver's threat against their
    rocky home.

What means the old Dominion? Hath she forgot the day
When o'er her conquered valleys swept the Briton's steel
    array?
How side by side, with sons of hers, the Massachusetts
    men
Encountered Tarleton's charge of fire, and stout
    Cornwallis, then?

Forgets she how the Bay State, in answer to the call
Of her old House of Burgesses, spoke out from Faneuil
    Hall?
When, echoing back her Henry's cry, came pulsing on
    each breath
Of Northern winds the thrilling sounds of 'LIBERTY OR
    DEATH!'

What asks the Old Dominion? If now her sons have
    proved
False to their fathers' memory—false to the faith they
    loved;
If she can scoff at Freedom, and its Great Charter spurn,
Must *we* of Massachusetts from Truth and Duty turn?

We hunt your bondmen, flying from Slavery's hateful
      hell—
Our voices, at your bidding, take up the bloodhounds'
      yell—
We gather, at your summons, above our fathers' graves,
From Freedom's holy altar horns to tear your wretched
      slaves!

Thank God! not yet so vilely can Massachusetts bow,
The spirit of her early time is with her even now;
Dream not because her pilgrim blood moves slow, and
      calm, and cool,
She thus can stoop her chainless neck, a sister's slave and
      tool!

All that a *sister* State should do, all that a *free* State may,
Heart, hand, and purse we proffer, as in our early day;
But that one dark loathsome burden, ye must stagger
      with alone,
And reap the bitter harvest which ye yourselves have
      sown!

Hold, while ye may, your struggling slaves, and burden
      God's free air
With woman's shriek beneath the lash, and manhood's
      wild despair;
Cling closer to the 'cleaving curse' that writes upon your
      plains,
The blasting of Almighty wrath against a land of chains.

Still shame your gallant ancestry, the cavaliers of old,
By watching round the *shambles* where human flesh is
    sold—
Gloat o'er the new-born child, and count his market
    value, when
The maddened mother's cry of woe shall pierce the
    slaver's den!

Lower than plummet soundeth, sink the Virginia name;
Plant, if ye will, your fathers' graves with rankest weeds
    of shame;
Be, if ye will, the scandal of God's fair universe—
We wash our hands forever, of your sin, and shame, and
    curse.

A voice from lips whereon the coal from Freedom's
    shrine hath been,
Thrilled, as but yesterday, the hearts of Berkshire's
    mountain men:
The echoes of that solemn voice are sadly lingering still
In all our sunny valleys, on every wind-swept hill.

And when the prowling man-thief came hunting for his
    prey
Beneath the very shadow of Bunker's shaft of grey,
How, through the free lips of the son, the father's
    warning spoke;
How, from its bonds of trade and sect, the Pilgrim city
    broke!

A hundred thousand right arms were lifted up on high,
A hundred thousand voices sent back their loud reply;
Through the thronged towns of Essex the startling
 summons rang,
And up from bench and loom and wheel her young
 mechanics sprang.

The voice of free, broad Middlesex—of thousands as of
 one—
The shaft of Bunker calling to that of Lexington—
From Norfolk's ancient villages; from Plymouth's rocky
 bound
To where Nantucket feels the arms of ocean close her
 round;

From rich and rural Worcester, where through the calm
 repose
Of cultured vales and fringing woods the gentle Nashua
 flows,
To where Wachusett's wintry blasts the mountain larches
 stir,
Swelled up to heaven the thrilling cry of 'God save
 Latimer!'

And sandy Barnstable rose up, wet with the salt sea
 spray—
And Bristol sent her answering shout down
 Narragansett Bay!

Along the broad Connecticut old Hampden felt the
      thrill,
And the cheer of Hampshire's woodmen swept down
      from Holyoke Hill.

The voice of Massachusetts! Of her free sons and
      daughters—
Deep calling unto deep aloud—the sound of many
      waters!
Against the burden of that voice what tyrant power shall
      stand?
No fetters in the Bay State! No slave upon her land!

Look to it well, Virginians! In calmness we have borne,
In answer to our faith and trust, your insult and your
      scorn;
You've spurned our kindest counsels—you've hunted for
      our lives—
And shaken round our hearths and homes your manacles
      and gyves!

We wage no war—we lift no arm—we fling no torch
      within
The fire-damps of the quaking mine beneath your soil of
      sin;
We leave ye with your bondmen—to wrestle, while ye
      can,
With the strong upward tendencies and God-like soul of
      man!

But for us and for our children, the vow which we have
    given
For Freedom and humanity is registered in Heaven:
No slave-hunt in our borders—no pirate on our strand!
No fetters in the Bay State—no slave upon our land!

Song of Slaves in the Desert

Where are we going? where are we going,
  Where are we going, Rubee?

Lord of peoples, lord of lands,
Look across these shining sands,
Through the furnace of the noon,
Through the white light of the moon.
Strong the Ghiblee wind is blowing,
Strange and large the world is growing!
Speak and tell us where we are going,
  Where are we going, Rubee?

Bornou land was rich and good,
Wells of water, fields of food,
Dourra fields, and bloom of bean,
And the palm-tree cool and green:
Bornou land we see no longer,
Here we thirst and here we hunger,
Here the Moor-man smites in anger:
  Where are we going, Rubee?

When we went from Bornou land,
We were like the leaves and sand,—
We were many, we are few;
Life has one, and death has two:
Whitened bones our path are showing,
Thou All-seeing, thou All-knowing!
Hear us, tell us where are we going,
    Where are we going, Rubee?

Moons of marches from our eyes
Bornou land behind us lies;
Stranger round us day by day
Bends the desert circle gray;
Wild the waves of sand are flowing,
Hot the winds above them blowing,—
Lord of all things!—where are we going?
    Where are we going, Rubee?

We are weak, but Thou art strong;
Short our lives, but Thine is long;
We are blind, but Thou hast eyes;
We are fools, but Thou art wise!
Thou, our morrow's pathway knowing
Through the strange world round us growing,
Hear us, tell us where are we going,
    Where are we going, Rubee?

The Huskers

It was late in mild October, and the long autumnal rain
Had left the summer harvest-fields all green with grass
      again;
The first sharp frosts had fallen, leaving all the
      woodlands gay
With the hues of summer's rainbow, or the meadow-
      flowers of May.

Through a thin, dry mist, that morning, the sun rose
      broad and red,
At first a rayless disc of fire, he brightened as he sped;
Yet, even his noontide glory fell chastened and subdued,
On the corn-fields and the orchards, and softly pictured
      wood.

And all that quiet afternoon, slow sloping to the night,
He wove with golden shuttle the haze with yellow light;
Slanting through the painted beeches, he glorified the
      hill;
And, beneath it, pond and meadow lay brighter, greener
      still.

And shouting boys in woodland haunts caught glimpses
      of that sky,
Flecked by the many-tinted leaves, and laughed, they
      knew not why;
And school-girls, gay with aster-flowers, beside the
      meadow brooks,
Mingled the glow of autumn with the sunshine of sweet
      looks.

From spire and barn, looked westerly the patient
     weathercocks;
But even the birches on the hill stood motionless as
     rocks.
No sound was in the woodlands, save the squirrel's
     dropping shell,
And the yellow leaves among the boughs, low rustling as
     they fell.

The summer grains were harvested; the stubble-fields
     lay dry,
Where June winds rolled, in light and shade, the pale-
     green waves of rye;
But still, on gentle hill-slopes, in valleys fringed with
     wood,
Ungathered, bleaching in the sun, the heavy corn crop
     stood.

Bent low, by autumn's wind and rain, through husks
     that, dry and sere,
Unfolded from their ripened charge, shone out the
     yellow ear;
Beneath, the turnip lay concealed, in many a verdant
     fold,
And glistened in the slanting light the pumpkin's sphere
     of gold.

There wrought the busy harvesters; and many a creaking
     wain
Bore slowly to the long barn-floor its load of husk and
     grain;

Till broad and red, as when he rose, the sun sank down,
     at last,
And like a merry guest's farewell, the day in brightness
     passed.

And lo! as through the western pines, on meadow,
     stream and pond,
Flamed the red radiance of a sky, set all afire beyond,
Slowly o'er the Eastern sea-bluffs a milder glory shone,
And the sunset and the moonrise were mingled into one!

As thus into the quiet night the twilight lapsed away,
And deeper in the brightening moon the tranquil
     shadows lay;
From many a brown old farm-house, and hamlet
     without name,
Their milking and their home-tasks done, the merry
     huskers came.

Swung o'er the heaped-up harvest, from pitchforks in
     the mow,
Shone dimly down the lanterns on the pleasant scene
     below;
The growing pile of husks behind, the golden ears
     before,
And laughing eyes and busy hands and brown cheeks
     glimmering o'er.

Half hidden, in a quiet nook, serene of look and heart,
Talking their old times over, the old men sat apart;

While, up and down the unhusked pile, or nestling in its
        shade,
At hide-and-seek, with laugh and shout, the happy
        children played.

Urged by the good host's daughter, a maiden young and
        fair,
Lifting to light her sweet blue eyes and pride of soft
        brown hair,
The master of the village school, sleek of hair and
        smooth of tongue,
To the quaint tune of some old psalm, a husking-ballad
        sung.

THE CORN SONG

Heap high the farmer's wintry hoard!
   Heap high the golden corn!
No richer gift has Autumn poured
   From out her lavish horn!

Let other lands, exulting, glean
   The apple from the pine,
The orange from its glossy green,
   The cluster from the vine;

We better love the hardy gift
   Our rugged vales bestow,
To cheer us when the storm shall drift
   Our harvest-fields with snow.

Through vales of grass and meads of flowers,
    Our ploughs their furrows made,
While on the hills the sun and showers
    Of changeful April played.

We dropped the seed o'er hill and plain,
    Beneath the sun of May,
And frightened from our sprouting grain
    The robber crows away.

All through the long, bright days of June,
    Its leaves grew green and fair,
And waved in hot midsummer's noon
    Its soft and yellow hair.

And now, with Autumn's moonlit eves,
    Its harvest time has come,
We pluck away the frosted leaves,
    And bear the treasure home.

There, richer than the fabled gift
    Apollo showered of old,
Fair hands the broken grain shall sift,
    And knead its meal of gold.

Let vapid idlers loll in silk,
    Around their costly board;
Give us the bowl of samp and milk,
    By homespun beauty poured!

Where'er the wide old kitchen hearth
    Sends up its smoky curls,
Who will not thank the kindly earth,
    And bless our farmer girls!

Then shame on all the proud and vain,
    Whose folly laughs to scorn
The blessing of our hardy grain,
    Our wealth of golden corn!

Let earth withhold her goodly root,
    Let mildew blight the rye,
Give to the worm the orchard's fruit,
    The wheat-field to the fly:

But let the good old crop adorn
    The hills our fathers trod;
Still let us, for His golden corn,
    Send up our thanks to God!

Proem

    I love the old melodious lays
Which softly melt the ages through,
    The songs of Spenser's golden days,
    Arcadian Sidney's silvery phrase,
Sprinkling our noon of time with freshest morning dew.

    Yet, vainly in my quiet hours
To breathe their marvellous notes I try;

I feel them, as the leaves and flowers
In silence feel the dewy showers,
And drink with glad still lips the blessing of the sky.

The rigor of a frozen clime,
The harshness of an untaught ear,
The jarring words of one whose rhyme
Beat often Labor's hurried time,
Or Duty's rugged march through storm and strife, are
here.

Of mystic beauty, dreamy grace,
No rounded art the lack supplies;
Unskilled the subtle lines to trace
Or softer shades of Nature's face,
I view her common forms with unanointed eyes.

Nor mine the seer-like power to show
The secrets of the heart and mind;
To drop the plummet-line below
Our common world of joy and woe,
A more intense despair or brighter hope to find.

Yet here at least an earnest sense
Of human right and weal is shown;
A hate of tyranny intense,
And hearty in its vehemence,
As if my brother's pain and sorrow were my own.

Oh Freedom! if to me belong
Nor mighty Milton's gift divine,

Nor Marvel's wit and graceful song,
  Still with a love as deep and strong
As theirs, I lay, like them, my best gifts on thy shrine!

Lines on the Portrait of a Celebrated Publisher

A moony breadth of virgin face,
  By thought unviolated;
A patient mouth, to take from scorn
  The hook with bank-notes baited!
Its self-complacent sleekness shows
  How thrift goes with the fawner—
An unctuous unconcern of all
  Which nice folks call dishonor!

A pleasant print to peddle out
  In lands of rice and cotton;
The model of that face in dough
  Would make the artist's fortune.
For Fame to thee has come unsought,
  While others vainly woo her,
In proof how mean a thing can make
  A great man of its doer.

To whom shall men thyself compare,
  Since common models fail 'em,
Save classic goose of ancient Rome,
  Or sacred ass of Balaam?
The gabble of that wakeful goose

Saved Rome from sack of Brennus;
The braying of the prophet's ass
  Betrayed the angel's menace!

So when Guy Fawkes, with silken shirt
  And azure-tinted hose on,
Was twisting from thy love-lorn sheets
  The slow-match of explosion—
An earthquake blast that would have tossed
  The Union as a feather,
Thy instinct saved a perilled land
  And perilled purse together.

Just think of Carolina's sage
  Sent whirling like a Dervish,
Of Quettlebum in middle air
  Performing strange drill-service!
Doomed like Assyria's lord of old,
  Who fell before the Jewess,
Or sad Abimelech, to sigh,
  "Alas! a woman slew us!"

Thou saw'st beneath a fair disguise
  The danger darkly working,
In flowing locks and laughing eyes
  The cunning mischief lurking.
How keen to scent the hidden plot!
  How prompt wert thou to balk it,
With patriot zeal and pedler thrift,
  For country and for pocket!

Thy likeness here is doubtless well,
    But higher honor 's due it;
On auction-block and negro-jail
    Admiring eyes should view it.
Or, hung aloft, it well might grace
    The nation's senate-chamber—
A greedy Northern bottle-fly
    Preserved in Slavery's amber!

Ichabod!

So fallen! so lost! the light withdrawn
    Which once he wore!
The glory from his gray hairs gone
    Forevermore!

Revile him not—the Tempter hath
    A snare for all;
And pitying tears, not scorn and wrath,
    Befit his fall!

Oh! dumb be passion's stormy rage,
    When he who might
Have lighted up and led his age,
    Falls back in night.

Scorn! would the angels laugh, to mark
    A bright soul driven,
Fiend-goaded, down the endless dark,
    From hope and heaven!

Let not the land, once proud of him,
    Insult him now,
Nor brand with deeper shame his dim,
    Dishonored brow.

But let its humbled sons, instead,
    From sea to lake,
A long lament, as for the dead,
    In sadness make.

Of all we loved and honored, nought
    Save power remains—
A fallen angel's pride of thought,
    Still strong in chains.

All else is gone; from those great eyes
    The soul has fled:
When faith is lost, when honor dies,
    The man is dead!

Then, pay the reverence of old days
    To his dead fame;
Walk backward, with averted gaze,
    And hide the shame!

A Sabbath Scene

Scarce had the solemn Sabbath-bell
   Ceased quivering in the steeple,
Scarce had the parson to his desk
   Walked stately through his people,

When down the summer shaded street
   A wasted female figure,
With dusky brow and naked feet,
   Came rushing wild and eager.

She saw the white spire through the trees,
   She heard the sweet hymn swelling;
O, pitying Christ! a refuge give
   That poor one in Thy dwelling!

Like a scared fawn before the hounds,
   Right up the aisle she glided,
While close behind her, whip in hand,
   A lank-haired hunter strided.

She raised a keen and bitter cry,
   To Heaven and Earth appealing;—
Were manhood's generous pulses dead?
   Had woman's heart no feeling?

A score of stout hands rose between
   The hunter and the flying;
Age clenched his staff, and maiden eyes
   Flashed tearful, yet defying.

"Who dares profane this house and day?"
  Cried out the angry pastor.
"Why, bless your soul, the wench 's a slave,
  And I'm her lord and master!

"I've law and gospel on my side,
  And who shall dare refuse me?"
Down came the parson, bowing low,
  "My good sir, pray excuse me!

"Of course I know your right divine
  To own and work and whip her;
Quick, deacon, throw that Polyglott
  Before the wench, and trip her!"

Plump dropped the holy tome, and o'er
  Its sacred pages stumbling,
Bound hand and foot, a slave once more,
  The hapless wretch lay trembling.

I saw the parson tie the knots,
  The while his flock addressing,
The Scriptural claims of slavery
  With text on text impressing.

"Although," said he, "on Sabbath day,
  All secular occupations
Are deadly sins, we must fulfil
  Our moral obligations:

"And this commends itself as one
    To every conscience tender;
As Paul sent back Onesimus,
    My Christian friends, we send her!"

Shriek rose on shriek,—the Sabbath air
    Her wild cries tore asunder;
I listened, with hushed breath, to hear
    God answering with his thunder!

All still!—the very altar's cloth
    Had smothered down her shrieking,
And, dumb, she turned from face to face,
    For human pity seeking!

I saw her dragged along the aisle,
    Her shackles harshly clanking;
I heard the parson, over all,
    The Lord devoutly thanking!

My brain took fire: "Is this," I cried,
    "The end of prayer and preaching?
Then down with pulpit, down with priest,
    And give us Nature's teaching!

"Foul shame and scorn be on ye all
    Who turn the good to evil,
And steal the Bible from the Lord,
    To give it to the Devil!

"Than garbled text or parchment law
   I own a statute higher;
And God is true, though every book
   And every man's a liar!"

Just then I felt the deacon's hand
   In wrath my coat-tail seize on;
I heard the priest cry "Infidel!"
   The lawyer mutter "Treason!"

I started up,—where now were church,
   Slave, master, priest and people?
I only heard the supper-bell,
   Instead of clanging steeple.

But, on the open window's sill,
   O'er which the white blooms drifted,
The pages of a good old Book
   The wind of summer lifted.

And flower and vine, like angel wings
   Around the Holy Mother,
Waved softly there, as if God's truth
   And Mercy kissed each other.

And freely from the cherry-bough
   Above the casement swinging,
With golden bosom to the sun,
   The oriole was singing.

As bird and flower made plain of old
  The lesson of the Teacher,
So now I heard the written Word
  Interpreted by Nature!

For to my ear methought the breeze
  Bore Freedom's blessed word on;
THUS SAITH THE LORD: BREAK EVERY YOKE,
  UNDO THE HEAVY BURDEN!

The Haschish

Of all that Orient lands can vaunt
  Of marvels with our own competing,
The strangest is the Haschish plant,
  And what will follow on its eating.

What pictures to the taster rise,
  Of Dervish or of Almeh dances!
Of Eblis, or of Paradise,
  Set all aglow with Houri glances!

The poppy visions of Cathay,
  The heavy beer-trance of the Suabian;
The wizard lights and demon play
  Of nights Walpurgis and Arabian!

The Mollah and the Christian dog
  Change place in mad metempsychosis;

The Muezzin climbs the synagogue,
  The Rabbi shakes his beard at Moses!

The Arab by his desert well
  Sits choosing from some Caliph's daughters,
And hears his single camel's bell
  Sound welcome to his regal quarters.

The Koran's reader makes complaint
  Of Shitan dancing on and off it;
The robber offers alms, the saint
  Drinks Tokay and blasphemes the Prophet!

Such scenes that Eastern plant awakes;
  But we have one ordained to beat it,
The Haschish of the West, which makes
  Or fools or knaves of all who eat it.

The preacher eats, and straight appears
  His Bible in a new translation;
Its angels negro overseers,
  And Heaven itself a snug plantation!

The man of peace, about whose dreams
  The sweet millennial angels cluster,
Tastes the mad weed, and plots and schemes,
  A raving Cuban filibuster!

The noisiest Democrat, with ease,
  It turns to Slavery's parish beadle;

The shrewdest statesman eats and sees
    Due southward point the polar needle.

The Judge partakes, and sits ere long
    Upon his bench a railing blackguard;
Decides off-hand that right is wrong,
    And reads the ten commandments backward!

O, potent plant! so rare a taste
    Has never Turk or Gentoo gotten;
The hempen Haschish of the East
    Is powerless to our Western Cotton!

Moloch in State Street

The moon has set: while yet the dawn
    Breaks cold and gray,
Between the midnight and the morn
    Bear off your prey!

On, swift and still!—the conscious street
    Is panged and stirred;
Tread light!—that fall of serried feet
    The dead have heard!

The first drawn blood of Freedom's veins
    Gushed where ye tread;
Lo! through the dusk the martyr-stains
    Blush darkly red!

Beneath the slowly waning stars
   And whitening day,
What stern and awful presence bars
   That sacred way?

What faces frown upon ye, dark
   With shame and pain?
Come these from Plymouth's Pilgrim bark?
   Is that young Vane?

Who, dimly beckoning, speed ye on
   With mocking cheer?
Lo! spectral Andros, Hutchinson,
   And Gage, are here!

For ready mart or favoring blast
   Through Moloch's fire
Flesh of his flesh, unsparing, passed
   The Tyrian sire.

Ye make that ancient sacrifice
   Of Man to Gain,
Your traffic thrives, where Freedom dies,
   Beneath the chain.

Ye sow to-day; your harvest scorn
   And hate, is near;
How, think ye freemen, mountain-born,
   The tale will hear?

Thank God! our mother State can yet
    Her fame retrieve;
To you and to your children let
    The scandal cleave.

Chain Hall and Pulpit, Court and Press,
    Make gods of gold;
Let honor, truth, and manliness,
    Like wares be sold.

Your hoards are great, your walls are strong,
    But God is just;
The gilded chambers built by wrong
    Invite the rust.

What! know ye not the gains of Crime
    Are dust and dross;
Its ventures on the waves of time
    Foredoom'd to loss!

And still the Pilgrim State remains
    What she hath been;
Her inland hills, her seaward plains,
    Still nurture men!

Nor wholly lost the fallen mart—
    Her olden blood
Through many a free and generous heart
    Still pours its flood.

That brave old blood, quick-flowing yet,
  Shall know no check,
Till a free people's foot is set
  On Slavery's neck.

Even now, the peal of bell and gun,
  And hills aflame,
Tell of the first great triumph won
  In Freedom's name.

The long night dies: the welcome gray
  Of dawn we see;
Speed up the heavens thy perfect day,
  God of the free!

1851

First-Day Thoughts

In calm and cool and silence, once again
  I find my old accustomed place among
  My brethren, where, perchance, no human tongue
  Shall utter words; where never hymn is sung,
  Nor deep-toned organ blown, nor censer swung,
Nor dim light falling through the pictured pane!
There, syllabled by silence, let me hear
The still small voice which reached the prophet's ear;
Read in my heart a still diviner law

Than Israel's leader on his tables saw!
There let me strive with each besetting sin,
    Recall my wandering fancies, and restrain
    The sore disquiet of a restless brain;
    And, as the path of duty is made plain,
May grace be given that I may walk therein,
    Not like the hireling, for his selfish gain,
With backward glances and reluctant tread,
Making a merit of his coward dread,—
    But, cheerful, in the light around me thrown,
    Walking as one to pleasant service led;
    Doing God's will as if it were my own,
Yet trusting not in mine, but in His strength alone!

The Kansas Emigrants

We cross the prairie as of old
    The pilgrims crossed the sea,
To make the West, as they the East,
    The homestead of the free!

We go to rear a wall of men
    On Freedom's southern line
And plant beside the cotton-tree
    The rugged Northern pine!

We're flowing from our native hills
    As our free rivers flow;
The blessing of our Mother-land
    Is on us as we go.

We go to plant her common schools
   On distant prairie swells,
And give the Sabbaths of the wild
   The music of her bells.

Upbearing, like the Ark of old,
   The Bible in our van,
We go to test the truth of God
   Against the fraud of man.

No pause, nor rest, save where the streams
   That feed the Kansas run,
Save where our Pilgrim gonfalon
   Shall flout the setting sun!

We'll tread the prairie as of old
   Our fathers sailed the sea,
And make the West, as they the East,
   The homestead of the free!

Maud Muller

Maud Muller, on a summer's day,
Raked the meadow sweet with hay.

Beneath her torn hat glowed the wealth
Of simple beauty and rustic health.

Singing, she wrought, and her merry glee
The mock-bird echoed from his tree.

But, when she glanced to the far-off town,
White from its hill-slope looking down,

The sweet song died, and a vague unrest
And a nameless longing filled her breast—

A wish, that she hardly dared to own,
For something better than she had known.

The Judge rode slowly down the lane,
Smoothing his horse's chestnut mane.

He drew his bridle in the shade
Of the apple-trees, to greet the maid,

And ask a draught from the spring that flowed
Through the meadow, across the road.

She stooped where the cool spring bubbled up,
And filled for him her small tin cup,

And blushed as she gave it, looking down
On her feet so bare, and her tattered gown.

"Thanks!" said the Judge, "a sweeter draught
From a fairer hand was never quaffed."

He spoke of the grass and flowers and trees,
Of the singing birds and the humming bees;

Then talked of the haying, and wondered whether
The cloud in the west would bring foul weather.

And Maud forgot her brier-torn gown,
And her graceful ankles bare and brown;

And listened, while a pleased surprise
Looked from her long-lashed hazel eyes.

At last, like one who for delay
Seeks a vain excuse, he rode away.

Maud Muller looked and sighed: "Ah, me!
That I the Judge's bride might be!

"He would dress me up in silks so fine,
And praise and toast me at his wine.

"My father should wear a broadcloth coat;
My brother should sail a painted boat.

"I'd dress my mother so grand and gay,
And the baby should have a new toy each day.

"And I'd feed the hungry and clothe the poor,
And all should bless me who left our door."

The Judge looked back as he climbed the hill,
And saw Maud Muller standing still.

"A form more fair, a face more sweet,
Ne'er hath it been my lot to meet.

"And her modest answer and graceful air
Show her wise and good as she is fair.

"Would she were mine, and I to-day,
Like her, a harvester of hay:

"No doubtful balance of rights and wrongs,
Nor weary lawyers with endless tongues,

"But low of cattle and song of birds,
And health and quiet and loving words."

But he thought of his sisters proud and cold,
And his mother vain of her rank and gold.

So, closing his heart, the Judge rode on,
And Maud was left in the field alone.

But the lawyers smiled that afternoon,
When he hummed in court an old love-tune;

And the young girl mused beside the well,
Till the rain on the unraked clover fell.

He wedded a wife of richest dower,
Who lived for fashion, as he for power.

Yet oft, in his marble hearth's bright glow,
He watched a picture come and go:

And sweet Maud Muller's hazel eyes
Looked out in their innocent surprise.

Oft, when the wine in his glass was red,
He longed for the wayside well instead;

And closed his eyes on his garnished rooms,
To dream of meadows and clover-blooms.

And the proud man sighed, with a secret pain:
"Ah, that I were free again!

"Free as when I rode that day,
Where the barefoot maiden raked her hay."

She wedded a man unlearned and poor,
And many children played round her door.

But care and sorrow, and child-birth pain,
Left their traces on heart and brain.

And oft, when the summer sun shone hot
On the new-mown hay in the meadow lot,

And she heard the little spring brook fall
Over the roadside, through the wall,

In the shade of the apple-tree again
She saw a rider draw his rein.

And, gazing down with timid grace,
She felt his pleased eyes read her face.

Sometimes her narrow kitchen walls
Stretched away into stately halls;

The weary wheel to a spinnet turned,
The tallow candle an astral burned,

And for him who sat by the chimney-lug,
Dozing and grumbling o'er pipe and mug,

A manly form at her side she saw,
And joy was duty and love was law.

Then she took up her burden of life again,
Saying only, "It might have been."

Alas for maiden, alas for Judge,
For rich repiner and household drudge!

God pity them both! and pity us all,
Who vainly the dreams of youth recall.

For of all sad words of tongue or pen,
The saddest are these: "It might have been!"

Ah, well! for us all some sweet hope lies
Deeply buried from human eyes;

And, in the hereafter, angels may
Roll the stone from its grave away!

The Fruit-Gift

Last night, just as the tints of autumn's sky
    Of sunset faded from our hills and streams,
    I sat, vague listening, lapped in twilight dreams,
To the leaf's rustle, and the cricket's cry.
Then, like that basket, flush with summer fruit,
Dropped by the angels at the Prophet's foot,
Came, unannounced, a gift of clustered sweetness,
    Full-orbed, and glowing with the prisoned beams
Of summery suns, and, rounded to completeness
By kisses of the south wind and the dew.
Thrilled with a glad surprise, methought I knew
The pleasure of the homeward-turning Jew,
When Eschol's clusters on his shoulders lay,
Dropping their sweetness on his desert way.

I said, "This fruit beseems no world of sin,
    Its parent vine, rooted in Paradise,
    O'ercrept the wall, and never paid the price
    Of the great mischief—an ambrosial tree,
Eden's exotic, somehow smuggled in,
    To keep the thorns and thistles company."

Perchance our frail, sad mother plucked in haste
    A single vine-slip as she passed the gate,
Where the dread sword, alternate, paled and burned,
    And the stern angel, pitying her fate,
Forgave the lovely trespasser, and turned
Aside his face of fire; and thus the waste
And fallen world hath yet its annual taste
Of primal good, to prove of sin the cost,
And show by one gleaned ear the mighty harvest lost.

The Barefoot Boy

    Blessings on thee, little man,
Barefoot boy, with cheek of tan!
With thy turned-up pantaloons,
And thy merry whistled tunes;
With thy red lip, redder still
Kissed by strawberries on the hill;
With the sunshine on thy face,
Through thy torn brim's jaunty grace:
From my heart I give thee joy—
I was once a barefoot boy!
Prince thou art—the grown-up man
Only is republican.
Let the million-dollared ride!
Barefoot, trudging at his side,
Thou hast more than he can buy,
In the reach of ear and eye—
Outward sunshine, inward joy:
Blessings on thee, barefoot boy!

O, for boyhood's painless play,
Sleep that wakes in laughing day,
Health that mocks the doctor's rules,
Knowledge never learned of schools,
Of the wild bee's morning chase,
Of the wild-flower's time and place,
Flight of fowl, and habitude
Of the tenants of the wood;
How the tortoise bears his shell,
How the woodchuck digs his cell,
And the ground-mole sinks his well;
How the robin feeds her young,
How the oriole's nest is hung;
Where the whitest lilies blow,
Where the freshest berries grow,
Where the ground-nut trails its vine,
Where the wood-grape's clusters shine;
Of the black wasp's cunning way,
Mason of his walls of clay,
And the architectural plans
Of gray, hornet artisans!—
For, eschewing books and tasks,
Nature answers all he asks;
Hand in hand with her he walks,
Face to face with her he talks,
Part and parcel of her joy,—
Blessings on the barefoot boy!

O, for boyhood's time of June,
Crowding years in one brief moon,
When all things I heard or saw

Me, their master, waited for.
I was rich in flowers and trees,
Humming-birds and honey-bees;
For my sport the squirrel played,
Plied the snouted mole his spade;
For my taste the blackberry cone
Purpled over hedge and stone;
Laughed the brook for my delight
Through the day and through the night,
Whispering at the garden wall,
Talked with me from fall to fall;
Mine the sand-rimmed pickerel pond,
Mine the walnut slopes beyond,
Mine, on bending orchard trees,
Apples of Hesperides!
Still, as my horizon grew,
Larger grew my riches too;
All the world I saw or knew
Seemed a complex Chinese toy,
Fashioned for a barefoot boy!

O, for festal dainties spread,
Like my bowl of milk and bread,—
Pewter spoon and bowl of wood,
On the door-stone, gray and rude!
O'er me, like a regal tent,
Cloudy-ribbed, the sunset bent,
Purple-curtained, fringed with gold,
Looped in many a wind-swung fold;
While for music came the play
Of the pied frogs' orchestra;

And, to light the noisy choir,
Lit the fly his lamp of fire.
I was monarch: pomp and joy
Waited on the barefoot boy!

Cheerily, then, my little man,
Live and laugh, as boyhood can!
Though the flinty slopes be hard,
Stubble-speared the new-mown sward,
Every morn shall lead thee through
Fresh baptisms of the dew;
Every evening from thy feet
Shall the cool wind kiss the heat:
All too soon these feet must hide
In the prison cells of pride,
Lose the freedom of the sod,
Like a colt's for work be shod,
Made to tread the mills of toil,
Up and down in ceaseless moil:
Happy if their track be found
Never on forbidden ground;
Happy if they sink not in
Quick and treacherous sands of sin.
Ah! that thou couldst know thy joy,
Ere it passes, barefoot boy!

Letter

From a missionary of the Methodist Episcopal Church South,
in Kansas, to a distinguished politician.

DOUGLAS MISSION, *August, 1854.*

Last week—the Lord be praised for all His mercies
To His unworthy servant!—I arrived
Safe at the Mission, *via* Westport; where
I tarried over night, to aid in forming
A Vigilance Committee, to send back,
In shirts of tar, and feather-doublets quilted
With forty stripes save one, all Yankee comers,
Uncircumcised and Gentile, aliens from
The Commonwealth of Israel, who despise
The prize of the high calling of the saints,
Who plant amidst this heathen wilderness
Pure gospel institutions, sanctified
By patriarchal use. The meeting opened
With prayer, as was most fitting. Half an hour,
Or thereaway, I groaned, and strove, and wrestled,
As Jacob did at Penuel, till the power
Fell on the people, and they cried 'Amen!'
"Glory to God!" and stamped and clapped their hands;
And the rough river boatmen wiped their eyes;
"Go it, old hoss!" they cried, and cursed the niggers—
Fulfilling thus the word of prophecy,
"Cursed be Canaan." After prayer, the meeting
Chose a committee—good and pious men—
A Presbyterian Elder, Baptist deacon,
A local preacher, three or four class-leaders,
Anxious inquirers, and renewed backsliders,
A score in all—to watch the river ferry,

(As they of old did watch the fords of Jordan.)
And cut off all those Yankee tongues refuse
The Shibboleth of the Nebraska bill.
And then, in answer to repeated calls,
I gave a brief account of what I saw
In Washington; and truly many hearts
Rejoiced to know the President, and you
And all the Cabinet regularly hear
The gospel message of a Sunday morning,
Drinking with thirsty souls of the sincere
Milk of the Word. Glory! Amen, and Selah!

Here, at the Mission, all things have gone well:
The brother who, throughout my absence, acted
As overseer, assures me that the crops
Never were better. I have lost one negro,
A first-rate hand, but obstinate and sullen.
He ran away some time last spring, and hid
In the river timber. There my Indian converts
Found him, and treed and shot him. For the rest,
The heathens round about begin to feel
The influence of our pious ministrations
And works of love; and some of them already
Have purchased negroes, and are settling down
As sober Christians! Bless the Lord for this!
I know it will rejoice you. You, I hear,
Are on the eve of visiting Chicago,
To fight with the wild beasts of Ephesus,
Long John, and Dutch Free-Soilers. May your arm
Be clothed with strength, and on your tongue be found
The sweet oil of persuasion. So desires
Your brother and co-laborer. Amen!

    P. S.   All's lost. Even while I write these lines,
The Yankee abolitionists are coming
Upon us like a flood—grim, stalwart men,
Each face set like a flint of Plymouth Rock
Against our institutions—staking out
Their farm lots on the wooded Wakarusa,
Or squatting by the mellow-bottomed Kansas;
The pioneers of mightier multitudes,
The small rain-patter, ere the thunder shower
Drowns the dry prairies. Hope from man is not.
Oh, for a quiet berth at Washington,
Snug naval chaplaincy, or clerkship, where
These rumors of free labor and free soil
Might never meet me more. Better to be
Door-keeper in the White House, than to dwell
Amidst these Yankee tents, that, whitening, show
On the green prairie like a fleet becalmed.
Methinks I hear a voice come up the river
From those far bayous, where the alligators
Mount guard around the camping filibusters:
"Shake off the dust of Kansas. Turn to Cuba—
(That golden orange just about to fall,
O'er-ripe, into the Democratic lap;)
Keep pace with Providence, or, as we say,
Manifest destiny. Go forth and follow
The message of *our* gospel, thither borne
Upon the point of Quitman's bowie-knife,
And the persuasive lips of Colt's revolvers.
There may'st thou, underneath thy vine and fig-tree,
Watch thy increase of sugar cane and negroes,
Calm as a patriarch in his eastern tent!"
Amen: So mote it be. So prays your friend.

Skipper Ireson's Ride

Of all the rides since the birth of time,
Told in story or sung in rhyme,—
On Apuleius's Golden Ass,
Or one-eyed Calendar's horse of brass,
Witch astride of a human hack,
Islam's prophet on Al-Borák,—
The strangest ride that ever was sped
Was Ireson's, out from Marblehead!
     Old Floyd Ireson, for his hard heart,
     Tarred and feathered and carried in a cart
       By the women of Marblehead!

Body of turkey, head of owl,
Wings a-droop like a rained-on fowl,
Feathered and ruffled in every part,
Skipper Ireson stood in the cart.
Scores of women, old and young,
Strong of muscle, and glib of tongue,
Pushed and pulled up the rocky lane,
Shouting and singing the shrill refrain:
     "Here's Flud Oirson, fur his horrd horrt,
     Torr'd an' futherr'd an' corr'd in a corrt
       By the women o' Morble'ead!"

Wrinkled scolds with hands on hips,
Girls in bloom of cheek and lips,
Wild-eyed, free-limbed, such as chase
Bacchus round some antique vase,
Brief of skirt, with ankles bare,

Loose of kerchief and loose of hair,
With conch-shells blowing and fish-horns' twang,
Over and over the Mænads sang:
    "Here's Flud Oirson, fur his horrd horrt,
    Torr'd an' futherr'd an' corr'd in a corrt
        By the women o' Morble'ead!"

Small pity for him!—He sailed away
From a leaking ship, in Chaleur Bay,—
Sailed away from a sinking wreck,
With his own town's-people on her deck!
"Lay by! lay by!" they called to him.
Back he answered, "Sink or swim!
Brag of your catch of fish again!"
And off he sailed through the fog and rain!
    Old Floyd Ireson, for his hard heart,
    Tarred and feathered and carried in a cart
        By the women of Marblehead!

Fathoms deep in dark Chaleur
That wreck shall lie forevermore.
Mother and sister, wife and maid,
Looked from the rocks of Marblehead
Over the moaning and rainy sea,—
Looked for the coming that might not be!
What did the winds and the sea-birds say
Of the cruel captain who sailed away?—
    Old Floyd Ireson, for his hard heart,
    Tarred and feathered and carried in a cart
        By the women of Marblehead!

Through the street, on either side,
Up flew windows, doors swung wide;
Sharp-tongued spinsters, old wives gray,
Treble lent the fish-horn's bray.
Sea-worn grandsires, cripple-bound,
Hulks of old sailors run aground,
Shook head, and fist, and hat, and cane,
And cracked with curses the hoarse refrain:
    "Here's Flud Oirson, fur his horrd horrt,
    Torr'd an' futherr'd an' corr'd in a corrt
      By the women o' Morble'ead!"

Sweetly along the Salem road
Bloom of orchard and lilac showed.
Little the wicked skipper knew
Of the fields so green and the sky so blue.
Riding there in his sorry trim,
Like an Indian idol glum and grim,
Scarcely he seemed the sound to hear
Of voices shouting far and near:
    "Here's Flud Oirson, fur his horrd horrt,
    Torr'd an' futherr'd an' corr'd in a corrt
      By the women o' Morble'ead!"

"Hear me, neighbors!" at last he cried,—
"What to me is this noisy ride?
What is the shame that clothes the skin
To the nameless horror that lives within?
Waking or sleeping, I see a wreck,
And hear a cry from a reeling deck!
Hate me and curse me,—I only dread

The hand of God and the face of the dead!"
 Said old Floyd Ireson, for his hard heart,
 Tarred and feathered and carried in a cart
  By the women of Marblehead!

Then the wife of the skipper lost at sea
Said, "God has touched him!—why should we?"
Said an old wife mourning her only son,
"Cut the rogue's tether and let him run!"
So with soft relentings and rude excuse,
Half scorn, half pity, they cut him loose,
And gave him a cloak to hide him in,
And left him alone with his shame and sin.
 Poor Floyd Ireson, for his hard heart,
 Tarred and feathered and carried in a cart
  By the women of Marblehead!

The Last Walk in Autumn

I

O'er the bare woods, whose outstretched hands
 Plead with the leaden heavens in vain,
I see, beyond the valley lands,
 The sea's long level dim with rain.
Around me all things, stark and dumb,
 Seem praying for the snows to come,
And, for the summer bloom and greenness gone,
With winter's sunset lights and dazzling morns atone.

II

Along the river's summer walk,
    The withered tufts of asters nod;
And trembles on its arid stalk
    The hoar plume of the golden-rod.
And on a ground of sombre fir,
And azure-studded juniper,
The silver birch its buds of purple shows,
And scarlet berries tell where bloomed the sweet wild
        rose!

III

With mingled sound of horns and bells,
    A far-heard clang, the wild geese fly,
Storm-sent, from Arctic moors and fells,
    Like a great arrow through the sky,
Two dusky lines converged in one,
Chasing the southward-flying sun;
While the brave snow-bird and the hardy jay
Call to them from the pines, as if to bid them stay.

IV

I passed this way a year ago:
    The wind blew south; the noon of day
Was warm as June's; and save that snow
    Flecked the low mountains far away,
And that the vernal-seeming breeze
Mocked faded grass and leafless trees,
I might have dreamed of summer as I lay,
Watching the fallen leaves with the soft wind at play.

V

Since then, the winter blasts have piled
    The white pagodas of the snow
On these rough slopes, and, strong and wild,
    Yon river, in its overflow
Of spring-time rain and sun, set free,
Crashed with its ices to the sea;
And over these gray fields, then green and gold,
The summer corn has waved, the thunder's organ rolled.

VI

Rich gift of God! A year of time!
    What pomp of rise and shut of day,
What hues wherewith our Northern clime
    Makes autumn's dropping woodlands gay,
What airs outblown from ferny dells,
And clover-bloom and sweet-brier smells,
What songs of brooks and birds, what fruits and flowers,
Green woods and moonlit snows, have in its round been
      ours!

VII

I know not how, in other lands,
    The changing seasons come and go;
What splendors fall on Syrian sands,
    What purple lights on Alpine snow!
Nor how the pomp of sunrise waits
On Venice at her watery gates;
A dream alone to me is Arno's vale,
And the Alhambra's halls are but a traveller's tale.

VIII

Yet, on life's current, he who drifts
    Is one with him who rows or sails;
And he who wanders widest, lifts
    No more of beauty's jealous veils
Than he who from his doorway sees
The miracle of flowers and trees,
Feels the warm Orient in the noonday air,
And from cloud minarets hears the sunset call to prayer!

IX

The eye may well be glad, that looks
    Where Pharpar's fountains rise and fall;
But he who sees his native brooks
    Laugh in the sun, has seen them all.
The marble palaces of Ind
Rise round him in the snow and wind;
From his lone sweet-brier Persian Hafiz smiles,
And Rome's cathedral awe is in his woodland aisles.

X

And thus it is my fancy blends
    The near at hand and far and rare;
And while the same horizon bends
    Above the silver-sprinkled hair
Which flashed the light of morning skies
On childhood's wonder-lifted eyes,
Within its round of sea and sky and field,
Earth wheels with all her zones, the Kosmos stands
        revealed.

XI

And thus the sick man on his bed,
  The toiler to his task-work bound,
Behold their prison-walls outspread,
  Their clipped horizon widen round!
While freedom-giving fancy waits,
  Like Peter's angel at the gates,
The power is theirs to baffle care and pain,
To bring the lost world back, and make it theirs again!

XII

What lack of goodly company,
  When masters of the ancient lyre
Obey my call, and trace for me
  Their words of mingled tears and fire!
I talk with Bacon, grave and wise,
I read the world with Pascal's eyes;
And priest and sage, with solemn brows austere,
And poets, garland-bound, the Lords of Thought, draw
    near.

XIII

Methinks, O friend, I hear thee say,
  "In vain the human heart we mock;
Bring living guests who love the day,
  Not ghosts who fly at crow of cock!
The herbs we share with flesh and blood,
Are better than ambrosial food,
With laurelled shades."   I grant it, nothing loth,
But doubly blest is he who can partake of both.

XIV

He who might Plato's banquet grace,
   Have I not seen before me sit,
And watched his puritanic face,
   With more than Eastern wisdom lit?
Shrewd mystic! who, upon the back
Of his Poor Richard's Almanack,
Writing the Sufi's song, the Gentoo's dream,
Links Manu's age of thought to Fulton's age of steam!

XV

Here too, of answering love secure,
   Have I not welcomed to my hearth
The gentle pilgrim troubadour,
   Whose songs have girdled half the earth;
Whose pages, like the magic mat
Whereon the Eastern lover sat,
Have borne me over Rhine-land's purple vines,
And Nubia's tawny sands, and Phrygia's mountain pines!

XVI

And he, who to the lettered wealth
   Of ages, adds the lore unpriced,
The wisdom and the moral health,
   The ethics of the school of Christ;
The statesman to his holy trust
As the Athenian archon just,
Struck down, exiled like him for truth alone,
Has he not graced my home with beauty all his own?

XVII

What greetings smile, what farewells wave,
　　What loved ones enter and depart!
The good, the beautiful, the brave,
　　The Heaven-lent treasures of the heart!
How conscious seems the frozen sod
And beechen slope whereon they trod!
The oak-leaves rustle, and the dry grass bends
Beneath the shadowy feet of lost or absent friends.

XVIII

Then ask not why to these bleak hills
　　I cling, as clings the tufted moss,
To bear the winter's lingering chills,
　　The mocking spring's perpetual loss.
I dream of lands where summer smiles,
　　And soft winds blow from spicy isles,
But scarce would Ceylon's breath of flowers be sweet,
Could I not feel thy soil, New England, at my feet!

XIX

At times I long for gentler skies,
　　And bathe in dreams of softer air,
But homesick tears would fill the eyes
　　That saw the Cross without the Bear.
The pine must whisper to the palm,
　　The north-wind break the tropic calm;
And with the dreamy languor of the Line,
The North's keen virtue blend, and strength to beauty
　　　　join.

XX

Better to stem with heart and hand
    The roaring tide of life, than lie,
Unmindful, on its flowery strand,
    Of God's occasions drifting by!
Better with naked nerve to bear
The needles of this goading air,
Than, in the lap of sensual ease, forego
The Godlike power to do, the Godlike aim to know.

XXI

Home of my heart! to me more fair
    Than gay Versailles or Windsor's halls,
The painted, shingly town-house where
    The freeman's vote for Freedom falls!
The simple roof where prayer is made,
    Than Gothic groin and colonnade;
The living temple of the heart of man,
Than Rome's sky-mocking vault, or many-spired Milan!

XXII

More dear thy equal village schools,
    Where rich and poor the Bible read,
Than classic halls where Priestcraft rules,
    And Learning wears the chains of Creed;
Thy glad Thanksgiving, gathering in
    The scattered sheaves of home and kin,
Than the mad license following Lenten pains,
Or holydays of slaves who laugh and dance in chains.

XXIII

And sweet homes nestle in these dales,
    And perch along these wooded swells;
And, blest beyond Arcadian vales,
    They hear the sound of Sabbath bells!
Here dwells no perfect man sublime,
    Nor woman winged before her time,
But with the faults and follies of the race,
Old home-bred virtues hold their not unhonored place.

XXIV

Here manhood struggles for the sake
    Of mother, sister, daughter, wife,
The graces and the loves which make
    The music of the march of life;
And woman, in her daily round
    Of duty, walks on holy ground.
No unpaid menial tills of soil, nor here
Is the bad lesson learned at human rights to sneer.

XXV

Then let the icy North wind blow
    The trumpets of the coming storm,
To arrowy sleet and blinding snow
    Yon slanting lines of rain transform.
Young hearts shall hail the drifted cold,
    As gayly as I did of old;
And I, who watch them through the frosty pane,
Unenvious, live in them my boyhood o'er again.

XXVI

And I will trust that He who heeds
  The life that hides in mead and wold,
Who hangs yon alder's crimson beads,
  And stains these mosses green and gold,
Will still, as He hath done, incline
His gracious care to me and mine;
Grant what we ask aright, from wrong debar,
And, as the earth grows dark, make brighter every star!

XXVII

I have not seen, I may not see,
  My hopes for man take form in fact,
But God will give the victory
  In due time; in that faith I act.
And he who sees the future sure,
  The baffling present may endure,
And bless, meanwhile, the unseen Hand that leads
The heart's desires beyond the halting step of deeds.

XXVIII

And thou, my song, I send thee forth,
  Where harsher songs of mine have flown;
Go, find a place at home and hearth
  Where'er thy singer's name is known;
Revive for him the kindly thought
  Of friends; and they who love him not,
Touched by some strain of thine, perchance may take
The hand he proffers all, and thank him for thy sake.

The Garrison of Cape Ann

From the hills of home forth looking, far beneath the
      tent-like span
Of the sky, I see the white gleam of the headland of
      Cape Ann.
Well I know its coves and beaches to the ebb-tide
      glimmering down,
And the white-walled hamlet children of its ancient
      fishing town.

Long has passed the summer morning, and its memory
      waxes old,
When along yon breezy headlands with a pleasant friend
      I strolled.
Ah! the autumn sun is shining, and the ocean wind
      blows cool,
And the golden-rod and aster bloom around thy grave,
      Rantoul!

With the memory of that morning by the summer sea I
      blend
A wild and wondrous story, by the younger Mather
      penned,
In that quaint *Magnalia Christi*, with all strange and
      marvellous things,
Heaped up huge and undigested, like the chaos Ovid
      sings.

Dear to me these far, faint glimpses of the dual life of
old,
Inward, grand with awe and reverence; outward, mean
and coarse and cold;
Gleams of mystic beauty playing over dull and vulgar
clay,
Golden threads of romance weaving in a web of hodden
gray.

The great eventful Present hides the Past; but through
the din
Of its loud life, hints and echoes from the life behind
steal in;
And the lore of home and fireside, and the legendary
rhyme,
Make the task of duty lighter which the true man owes
his time.

So, with something of the feeling which the Covenanter
knew,
When the pious chisel wandering Scotland's moorland
graveyards through,
From the graves of old traditions I part the blackberry
vines,
Wipe the moss from off the headstones, and retouch the
faded lines.

———

Where the sea-waves back and forward, hoarse with
rolling pebbles, ran,
The garrison-house stood watching on the gray rocks of
Cape Ann;

On its windy site uplifting gabled roof and palisade,
And rough walls of unhewn timber with the moonlight
overlaid.

On his slow round walked the sentry, south and eastward
looking forth
O'er a rude and broken coast-line, white with breakers
stretching north,—
Wood and rock and gleaming sand-drift, jagged capes,
with bush and tree,
Leaning inland from the smiting of the wild and gusty
sea.

Before the deep-mouthed chimney, dimly lit by dying
brands,
Twenty soldiers sat and waited, with their muskets in
their hands;
On the rough-hewn oaken table the venison haunch was
shared,
And the pewter tankard circled slowly round from beard
to beard.

Long they sat and talked together,—talked of wizards
Satan-sold;
Of all ghostly sights and noises,—signs and wonders
manifold;
Of the spectre-ship of Salem, with the dead men in her
shrouds,
Sailing sheer above the water, in the loom of morning
clouds;

Of the marvellous valley hidden in the depth of
        Gloucester woods,
Full of plants that love the summer—blooms of warmer
        latitudes;
Where the Arctic birch is braided by the tropic's flowery
        vines,
And the white magnolia blossoms star the twilight of the
        pines!

But their voices sank yet lower, sank to husky tones of
        fear,
As they spake of present tokens of the powers of evil
        near;
Of a spectral host, defying stroke of steel and aim of
        gun;
Never yet was ball to slay them in the mould of mortals
        run!

Thrice, with plumes of flowing scalp-locks, from the
        midnight wood they came,—
Thrice around the block-house marching, met,
        unharmed, its volleyed flame;
Then, with mocking laugh and gesture, sunk in earth or
        lost in air,
All the ghostly wonder vanished, and the moon-lit sands
        lay bare.

Midnight came; from out the forest moved a dusky
        mass, that soon
Grew to warriors, plumed and painted, grimly marching
        in the moon.

"Ghosts or witches," said the captain, "thus I foil the
    Evil One!"
And he rammed a silver button, from his doublet, down
    his gun.

Once again the spectral horror moved the guarded wall
    about;
Once again the levelled muskets through the palisades
    flashed out,
With that deadly aim the squirrel on his tree-top might
    not shun,
Nor the beach-bird seaward flying with his slant wing to
    the sun.

Like the idle rain of summer sped the harmless shower
    of lead.
With a laugh of fierce derision, once again the phantoms
    fled;
Once again, without a shadow on the sands the
    moonlight lay,
And the white smoke curling through it drifted slowly
    down the bay!

"God preserve us!" said the captain; "never mortal foes
    were there;
They have vanished with their leader, Prince and Power
    of the Air!
Lay aside your useless weapons; skill and prowess naught
    avail;
They who do the devil's service, wear their master's coat
    of mail!"

So the night grew near to cock-crow, when again a
        warning call
Roused the score of weary soldiers watching round the
        dusky hall.
And they looked to flint and priming, and they longed
        for break of day;
But the captain closed his Bible: "Let us cease from man,
        and pray!"

To the men who went before us, all the unseen powers
        seemed near,
And their steadfast strength of courage struck its roots in
        holy fear.
Every hand forsook the musket, every head was bowed
        and bare,
Every stout knee pressed the flag-stones, as the captain
        led in prayer.

Ceased thereat the mystic marching of the spectres
        round the wall,
But a sound abhorred, unearthly, smote the ears and
        hearts of all,—
Howls of rage and shrieks of anguish! Never after
        mortal man
Saw the ghostly leaguers marching round the block-
        house of Cape Ann.

So to us who walk in summer through the cool and sea-
        blown town,
From the childhood of its people comes the solemn
        legend down.

Not in vain the ancient fiction, in whose moral lives the
  youth
And the fitness and the freshness of an undecaying truth.

Soon or late to all our dwellings come the spectres of the
  mind,
Doubts and fears and dread forebodings, in the darkness
  undefined;
Round us throng the grim projections of the heart and
  of the brain,
And our pride of strength is weakness, and the cunning
  hand is vain.

In the dark we cry like children; and no answer from on
  high
Breaks the crystal spheres of silence, and no white wings
  downward fly;
But the heavenly help we pray for comes to faith, and
  not to sight,
And our prayers themselves drive backward all the spirits
  of the night!

Telling the Bees

Here is the place; right over the hill
  Runs the path I took;
You can see the gap in the old wall still,
  And the stepping-stones in the shallow brook.

There is the house, with the gate red-barred,
    And the poplars tall;
And the barn's brown length, and the cattle-yard,
    And the white horns tossing above the wall.

There are the bee-hives ranged in the sun;
    And down by the brink
Of the brook are her poor flowers, weed-o'errun,
    Pansy and daffodil, rose and pink.

A year has gone, as the tortoise goes,
    Heavy and slow;
And the same rose blows, and the same sun glows,
    And the same brook sings of a year ago.

There's the same sweet clover-smell in the breeze;
    And the June sun warm
Tangles his wings of fire in the trees,
    Setting, as then, over Fernside farm.

I mind me how with a lover's care
    From my Sunday coat
I brushed off the burs, and smoothed my hair,
    And cooled at the brook-side my brow and throat.

Since we parted, a month had passed,—
    To love, a year;
Down through the beeches I looked at last
    On the little red gate and the well-sweep near.

I can see it all now,—the slantwise rain
    Of light through the leaves,
The sundown's blaze on her window-pane,
    The bloom of her roses under the eaves.

Just the same as a month before,—
    The house and the trees,
The barn's brown gable, the vine by the door,—
    Nothing changed but the hives of bees.

Before them, under the garden wall,
    Forward and back,
Went drearily singing the chore-girl small,
    Draping each hive with a shred of black.

Trembling, I listened: the summer sun
    Had the chill of snow;
For I knew she was telling the bees of one
    Gone on the journey we all must go!

Then I said to myself, "My Mary weeps
    For the dead to-day:
Haply her blind old grandsire sleeps
    The fret and the pain of his age away."

But her dog whined low; on the doorway sill,
    With his cane to his chin,
The old man sat; and the chore-girl still
    Sung to the bees stealing out and in.

And the song she was singing ever since
    In my ear sounds on:—
"Stay at home, pretty bees, fly not hence!
    Mistress Mary is dead and gone!"

My Playmate

The pines were dark on Ramoth hill,
    Their song was soft and low;
The blossoms in the sweet May wind
    Were falling like the snow.

The blossoms drifted at our feet,
    The orchard birds sang clear;
The sweetest and the saddest day
    It seemed of all the year.

For, more to me than birds or flowers,
    My playmate left her home,
And took with her the laughing spring,
    The music and the bloom.

She kissed the lips of kith and kin,
    She laid her hand in mine:
What more could ask the bashful boy
    Who fed her father's kine?

She left us in the bloom of May:
  The constant years told o'er
Their seasons with as sweet May morns,
  But she came back no more.

I walk, with noiseless feet, the round
  Of uneventful years;
Still o'er and o'er I sow the spring
  And reap the autumn ears.

She lives where all the golden year
  Her summer roses blow;
The dusky children of the sun
  Before her come and go.

There haply with her jewelled hands
  She smooths her silken gown,—
No more the homespun lap wherein
  I shook the walnuts down.

The wild grapes wait us by the brook,
  The brown nuts on the hill,
And still the May-day flowers make sweet
  The woods of Follymill.

The lilies blossom in the pond,
  The bird builds in the tree,
The dark pines sing on Ramoth hill
  The slow song of the sea.

I wonder if she thinks of them,
   And how the old time seems,—
If ever the pines of Ramoth wood
   Are sounding in her dreams.

I see her face, I hear her voice:
   Does she remember mine?
And what to her is now the boy
   Who fed her father's kine?

What cares she that the orioles build
   For other eyes than ours,—
That other hands with nuts are filled,
   And other laps with flowers?

O playmate in the golden time!
   Our mossy seat is green,
Its fringing violets blossom yet,
   The old trees o'er it lean.

The winds so sweet with birch and fern
   A sweeter memory blow;
And there in spring the veeries sing
   The song of long ago.

And still the pines of Ramoth wood
   Are moaning like the sea,—
The moaning of the sea of change
   Between myself and thee!

The River Path

No bird-song floated down the hill;
The tangled bank below was still;

No rustle from the birchen stem,
No ripple from the water's hem.

The dusk of twilight round us grew;
We felt the fading of the dew;

For from us, ere the day was done,
The wooded hills shut out the sun.

But on the river's farther side
We saw the hill tops glorified,

A tender glow, exceeding fair,
A dream of day without its glare.

With us the damp, the chill, the gloom;
With them the sunset's rosy bloom;

While dark, through willowy vistas seen,
The river rolled in shade between.

From out the darkness where we trod
We gazed upon those hills of God,

Whose light seemed not of moon or sun;
We spake not, but our thought was one.

We paused, as if from that bright shore
Beckoned our dear ones gone before;

And still our beating hearts to hear
The voices lost to mortal ear!

Sudden our pathway turned from night;
The hills swung open to the light;

Through their green gates the sunshine showed,
A long slant splendor downward flowed.

Down glade and glen and bank it rolled;
It bridged the shady stream with gold;

And, borne on piers of mist, allied
The shadowy with the sunlit side!

"So," prayed we, "when our feet draw near
The river, dark with mortal fear,

"And the night cometh chill with dew,
O Father! let thy light break through!

"So let the hills of doubt divide,
So bridge with faith the sunless tide!

"So let the eyes that fail on earth
On thy eternal hills look forth!

"And in thy beckoning angels know
The dear ones whom we loved below."

"Ein feste Burg ist unser Gott"

(Luther's Hymn.)

We wait beneath the furnace blast
  The pangs of transformation;
Not painlessly doth God recast
  And mould anew the nation.
    Hot burns the fire
    Where wrongs expire;
    Nor spares the hand
    That from the land
  Uproots the ancient evil.

The hand-breadth cloud the sages feared,
  Its bloody rain is dropping;
The poison plant the fathers spared,
  All else is overtopping.
    East, West, South, North,
    It curses the earth:
    All justice dies,
    And fraud and lies
  Live only in its shadow.

What gives the wheat field blades of steel?
  What points the rebel cannon?
What sets the roaring rabble's heel
  On the old star-spangled pennon?
    What breaks the oath
    Of the men o' the South?
    What whets the knife
    For the Union's life?—
  Hark to the answer:—SLAVERY!

Then waste no blows on lesser foes,
    In strife unworthy freemen.
God lifts to-day the veil, and shows
    The features of the demon!
        O North and South,
        Its victims both,
        Can ye not cry,
        "Let Slavery die!"
    And union find in freedom?

What though the cast-out spirit tear
    The nation in his going?
We who have shared the guilt, must share
    The pang of his o'erthrowing!
        Whate'er the loss,
        Whate'er the cross,
        Shall they complain
        Of present pain,
    Who trust in God's hereafter?

For who that leans on His right arm,
    Was ever yet forsaken?
What righteous cause can suffer harm,
    If He its part has taken?
        Though wild and loud,
        And dark the cloud,
        Behind its folds
        His hand upholds
    The calm sky of to-morrow!

Above the maddening cry for blood,
    Above the wild war-drumming,

Let Freedom's voice be heard, with good
   The evil overcoming.
     Give prayer and purse
     To stay The Curse,
     Whose wrong we share,
     Whose shame we bear,
   Whose end shall gladden Heaven!

In vain the bells of war shall ring
   Of triumphs and revenges,
While still is spared the evil thing
   That severs and estranges.
     But, blest the ear
     That yet shall hear
     The jubilant bell
     That rings the knell
   Of Slavery forever!

Then let the selfish lip be dumb,
   And hushed the breath of sighing;
Before the joy of peace must come
   The pains of purifying.
     God give us grace,
     Each in his place
     To bear his lot,
     And, murmuring not,
   Endure, and wait, and labor!

The Waiting

I wait and watch: before my eyes
    Methinks the night grows thin and gray;
I wait and watch the eastern skies
To see the golden spears uprise
    Beneath the oriflamme of day!

Like one whose limbs are bound in trance
    I hear the day sounds swell and grow,
And see across the twilight glance,
Troop after troop, in swift advance,
    The shining ones with plumes of snow!

I know the errand of their feet,
    I know what mighty work is theirs;
I can but lift up hands unmeet,
The threshing-floors of God to beat,
    And speed them with unworthy prayers.

I will not dream in vain despair
    The steps of progress wait for me:
The puny leverage of a hair
The planet's impulse well may spare,
    A drop of dew the tided sea.

The loss, if loss there be, is mine,
    And yet not mine if understood;
For one shall grasp and one resign,
One drink life's rue, and one its wine,
    And God shall make the balance good.

O power to do! O baffled will!
    O prayer and action! ye are one;
Who may not strive, may yet fulfil
The harder task of standing still,
    And good but wished with God is done!

Barbara Frietchie

Up from the meadows rich with corn,
Clear in the cool September morn,

The clustered spires of Frederick stand
Green-walled by the hills of Maryland.

Round about them orchards sweep,
Apple- and peach-tree fruited deep,

Fair as a garden of the Lord
To the eyes of the famished rebel horde,

On that pleasant morn of the early fall
When Lee marched over the mountain wall,—

Over the mountains winding down,
Horse and foot, into Frederick town.

Forty flags with their silver stars,
Forty flags with their crimson bars,

Flapped in the morning wind: the sun
Of noon looked down, and saw not one.

Up rose old Barbara Frietchie then,
Bowed with her fourscore years and ten;

Bravest of all in Frederick town,
She took up the flag the men hauled down;

In her attic-window the staff she set,
To show that one heart was loyal yet.

Up the street came the rebel tread,
Stonewall Jackson riding ahead.

Under his slouched hat left and right
He glanced: the old flag met his sight.

"Halt!"—the dust-brown ranks stood fast.
"Fire!"—out blazed the rifle-blast.

It shivered the window, pane and sash;
It rent the banner with seam and gash.

Quick, as it fell, from the broken staff
Dame Barbara snatched the silken scarf;

She leaned far out on the window-sill,
And shook it forth with a royal will.

"Shoot, if you must, this old gray head,
But spare your country's flag," she said.

A shade of sadness, a blush of shame,
Over the face of the leader came;

The nobler nature within him stirred
To life at the woman's deed and word:

"Who touches a hair of yon gray head
Dies like a dog! March on!" he said.

All day long through Frederick street
Sounded the tread of marching feet:

All day long that free flag tost
Over the heads of the rebel host.

Ever its torn fields rose and fell
On the loyal winds that loved it well;

And through the hill-gaps sunset light
Shone over it with a warm good-night.

Barbara Frietchie's work o'er,
And the Rebel rides on his raids no more.

Honor to her! and let a tear
Fall, for her sake, on Stonewall's bier.

Over Barbara Frietchie's grave
Flag of Freedom and Union, wave!

Peace and order and beauty draw
Round thy symbol of light and law;

And ever the stars above look down
On thy stars below in Frederick town!

The Vanishers

Sweetest of all childlike dreams
   In the simple Indian lore
Still to me the legend seems
   Of the shapes who flit before.

Flitting, passing, seen and gone,
   Never reached nor found at rest,
Baffling search, but beckoning on
   To the Sunset of the Blest.

From the clefts of mountain rocks,
   Through the dark of lowland firs,
Flash the eyes and flow the locks
   Of the mystic Vanishers!

And the fisher in his skiff,
   And the hunter on the moss,
Hear their call from cape and cliff,
   See their hands the birch-leaves toss.

Wistful, longing, through the green
  Twilight of the clustered pines,
In their faces rarely seen
  Beauty more than mortal shines.

Fringed with gold their mantles flow
  On the slopes of westering knolls;
In the wind they whisper low
  Of the Sunset Land of Souls.

Doubt who may, O friend of mine!
  Thou and I have seen them too;
On before with beck and sign
  Still they glide, and we pursue.

More than clouds of purple trail
  In the gold of setting day;
More than gleams of wing or sail
  Beckon from the sea-mist gray.

Glimpses of immortal youth,
  Gleams and glories seen and flown,
Far-heard voices sweet with truth,
  Airs from viewless Eden blown,—

Beauty that eludes our grasp,
  Sweetness that transcends our taste,
Loving hands we may not clasp,
  Shining feet that mock our haste,—

Gentle eyes we closed below,
    Tender voices heard once more,
Smile and call us, as they go
    On and onward, still before.

Guided thus, O friend of mine!
    Let us walk our little way,
Knowing by each beckoning sign
    That we are not quite astray.

Chase we still with baffled feet,
    Smiling eye and waving hand,
Sought and seeker soon shall meet,
    Lost and found, in Sunset Land!

What the Birds Said

The birds against the April wind
    Flew northward, singing as they flew;
They sang, "The land we leave behind
    Has swords for corn-blades, blood for dew."

"O wild-birds, flying from the South,
    What saw and heard ye, gazing down?"
"We saw the mortar's upturned mouth,
    The sickened camp, the blazing town!

"Beneath the bivouac's starry lamps,
    We saw your march-worn children die;

In shrouds of moss, in cypress swamps,
    We saw your dead uncoffined lie.

"We heard the starving prisoner's sighs,
    And saw, from line and trench, your sons
Follow our flight with home-sick eyes
    Beyond the battery's smoking guns."

"And heard and saw ye only wrong
    And pain," I cried, "O wing-worn flocks?"
"We heard," they sang, "the freedman's song,
    The crash of Slavery's broken locks!

"We saw from new, uprising States
    The treason-nursing mischief spurned,
As, crowding Freedom's ample gates,
    The long-estranged and lost returned.

"O'er dusky faces, seamed and old,
    And hands horn-hard with unpaid toil,
With hope in every rustling fold,
    We saw your star-dropt flag uncoil.

"And struggling up through sounds accursed,
    A grateful murmur clomb the air;
A whisper scarcely heard at first,
    It filled the listening heavens with prayer.

"And sweet and far, as from a star,
    Replied a voice which shall not cease,

Till, drowning all the noise of war,
　　It sings the blessed song of peace!"

So to me, in a doubtful day
　　Of chill and slowly greening spring,
Low stooping from the cloudy gray,
　　The wild-birds sang or seemed to sing.

They vanished in the misty air,
　　The song went with them in their flight;
But lo! they left the sunset fair,
　　And in the evening there was light.

Laus Deo

On hearing the bells ring for the constitutional amendment
abolishing slavery in the United States.

　　　　It is done!
　　Clang of bell and roar of gun
Send the tidings up and down.
　　How the belfries rock and reel,
　　How the great guns, peal on peal,
Fling the joy from town to town!

　　　　Ring, O bells!
　　Every stroke exulting tells
Of the burial hour of crime.
　　Loud and long, that all may hear,
　　Ring for every listening ear
Of Eternity and Time!

Let us kneel:
God's own voice is in that peal,
And this spot is holy ground.
Lord, forgive us! What are we,
That our eyes this glory see,
That our ears have heard the sound!

For the Lord
On the whirlwind is abroad;
In the earthquake he has spoken;
He has smitten with his thunder
The iron walls asunder,
And the gates of brass are broken!

Loud and long
Lift the old exulting song,
Sing with Miriam by the sea:
He has cast the mighty down;
Horse and rider sink and drown;
He has triumphed gloriously!

Did we dare,
In our agony of prayer,
Ask for more than he has done?
When was ever his right hand
Over any time or land
Stretched as now beneath the sun!

How they pale,
Ancient myth, and song, and tale,
In this wonder of our days,

When the cruel rod of war
   Blossoms white with righteous law,
And the wrath of man is praise.

    Blotted out!
  All within and all about
Shall a fresher life begin;
   Freer breathe the universe
   As it rolls its heavy curse
On the dead and buried sin.

    It is done!
  In the circuit of the sun
Shall the sound thereof go forth.
   It shall bid the sad rejoice,
   It shall give the dumb a voice,
It shall belt with joy the earth!

    Ring and swing
  Bells of joy! on morning's wing
Send the song of praise abroad;
   With a sound of broken chains,
   Tell the nations that He reigns,
Who alone is Lord and God!

The Eternal Goodness

O friends! with whom my feet have trod
   The quiet aisles of prayer,
Glad witness to your zeal for God
   And love of man I bear.

I trace your lines of argument;
   Your logic linked and strong
I weigh as one who dreads dissent,
   And fears a doubt as wrong.

But still my human hands are weak
   To hold your iron creeds;
Against the words ye bid me speak
   My heart within me pleads.

Who fathoms the Eternal Thought?
   Who talks of scheme and plan?
The Lord is God! He needeth not
   The poor device of man.

I walk with bare, hushed feet the ground
   Ye tread with boldness shod;
I dare not fix with mete and bound
   The love and power of God.

Ye praise His justice; even such
   His pitying love I deem:
Ye seek a king; I fain would touch
   The robe that hath no seam.

Ye see the curse which overbroods
　　A world of pain and loss;
I hear our Lord's beatitudes
　　And prayer upon the cross.

More than your schoolmen teach, within
　　Myself, alas! I know;
Too dark ye cannot paint the sin,
　　Too small the merit show.

I bow my forehead to the dust,
　　I veil mine eyes for shame,
And urge, in trembling self-distrust,
　　A prayer without a claim.

I see the wrong that round me lies,
　　I feel the guilt within;
I hear, with groan and travail-cries,
　　The world confess its sin.

Yet, in the maddening maze of things,
　　And tossed by storm and flood,
To one fixed stake my spirit clings:
　　I know that God is good!

Not mine to look where cherubim
　　And seraphs may not see,
But nothing can be good in Him
　　Which evil is in me.

The wrong that pains my soul below
  I dare not throne above:
I know not of His hate,—I know
  His goodness and His love.

I dimly guess from blessings known
  Of greater out of sight,
And, with the chastened Psalmist, own
  His judgments too are right.

I long for household voices gone,
  For vanished smiles I long,
But God hath led my dear ones on,
  And He can do no wrong.

I know not what the future hath
  Of marvel or surprise,
Assured alone that life and death
  His mercy underlies.

And if my heart and flesh are weak
  To bear an untried pain,
The bruised reed He will not break,
  But strengthen and sustain.

No offering of my own I have,
  Nor works my faith to prove;
I can but give the gifts He gave,
  And plead His love for love.

And so beside the Silent Sea
    I wait the muffled oar;
No harm from Him can come to me
    On ocean or on shore.

I know not where His islands lift
    Their fronded palms in air;
I only know I cannot drift
    Beyond His love and care.

O brothers! if my faith is vain,
    If hopes like these betray,
Pray for me that my feet may gain
    The sure and safer way.

And Thou, O Lord! by whom are seen
    Thy creatures as they be,
Forgive me if too close I lean
    My human heart on Thee!

Snow-Bound

The sun that brief December day
Rose cheerless over hills of gray,
And, darkly circled, gave at noon
A sadder light than waning moon.
Slow tracing down the thickening sky
Its mute and ominous prophecy,
A portent seeming less than threat,
It sank from sight before it set.

A chill no coat, however stout,
Of homespun stuff could quite shut out,
A hard, dull bitterness of cold,
    That checked, mid-vein, the circling race
    Of life-blood in the sharpened face,
The coming of the snow-storm told.
The wind blew east: we heard the roar
Of Ocean on his wintry shore,
And felt the strong pulse throbbing there
Beat with low rhythm our inland air.

Meanwhile we did our nightly chores,—
Brought in the wood from out of doors,
Littered the stalls, and from the mows
Raked down the herd's-grass for the cows;
Heard the horse whinnying for his corn;
And, sharply clashing horn on horn,
Impatient down the stanchion rows
The cattle shake their walnut bows;
While, peering from his early perch
Upon the scaffold's pole of birch,
The cock his crested helmet bent
And down his querulous challenge sent.

Unwarmed by any sunset light
The gray day darkened into night,
A night made hoary with the swarm
And whirl-dance of the blinding storm,
As zigzag wavering to and fro
Crossed and recrossed the wingéd snow:
And ere the early bed-time came

The white drift piled the window-frame,
And through the glass the clothes-line posts
Looked in like tall and sheeted ghosts.

So all night long the storm roared on:
The morning broke without a sun;
In tiny spherule traced with lines
Of Nature's geometric signs,
In starry flake, and pellicle,
All day the hoary meteor fell;
And, when the second morning shone,
We looked upon a world unknown,
On nothing we could call our own.
Around the glistening wonder bent
The blue walls of the firmament,
No cloud above, no earth below,—
A universe of sky and snow!
The old familiar sights of ours
Took marvellous shapes; strange domes and towers
Rose up where sty or corn-crib stood,
Or garden wall, or belt of wood;
A smooth white mound the brush-pile showed,
A fenceless drift what once was road;
The bridle-post an old man sat
With loose-flung coat and high cocked hat;
The well-curb had a Chinese roof;
And even the long sweep, high aloof,
In its slant splendor, seemed to tell
Of Pisa's leaning miracle.

A prompt, decisive man, no breath
Our father wasted: "Boys, a path!"
Well pleased, (for when did farmer boy
Count such a summons less than joy?)
Our buskins on our feet we drew;
    With mittened hands, and caps drawn low,
    To guard our necks and ears from snow,
We cut the solid whiteness through.
And, where the drift was deepest, made
A tunnel walled and overlaid
With dazzling crystal: we had read
Of rare Aladdin's wondrous cave,
And to our own his name we gave,
With many a wish the luck were ours
To test his lamp's supernal powers.
We reached the barn with merry din,
And roused the prisoned brutes within.
The old horse thrust his long head out,
And grave with wonder gazed about;
The cock his lusty greeting said,
And forth his speckled harem led;
The oxen lashed their tails, and hooked,
And mild reproach of hunger looked;
The hornéd patriarch of the sheep,
Like Egypt's Amun roused from sleep,
Shook his sage head with gesture mute,
And emphasized with stamp of foot.

All day the gusty north-wind bore
The loosening drift its breath before;
Low circling round its southern zone,

The sun through dazzling snow-mist shone.
No church-bell lent its Christian tone
To the savage air, no social smoke
Curled over woods of snow-hung oak.
A solitude made more intense
By dreary voicéd elements,
The shrieking of the mindless wind,
The moaning tree-boughs swaying blind,
And on the glass the unmeaning beat
Of ghostly finger-tips of sleet.
Beyond the circle of our hearth
No welcome sound of toil or mirth
Unbound the spell, and testified
Of human life and thought outside.
We minded that the sharpest ear
The buried brooklet could not hear,
The music of whose liquid lip
Had been to us companionship,
And, in our lonely life, had grown
To have an almost human tone.

As night drew on, and, from the crest
Of wooded knolls that ridged the west,
The sun, a snow-blown traveller, sank
From sight beneath the smothering bank,
We piled, with care, our nightly stack
Of wood against the chimney-back,—
The oaken log, green, huge, and thick,
And on its top the stout back-stick;
The knotty forestick laid apart,
And filled between with curious art

The ragged brush; then, hovering near,
We watched the first red blaze appear,
Heard the sharp crackle, caught the gleam
On whitewashed wall and sagging beam,
Until the old, rude-furnished room
Burst, flower-like, into rosy bloom;
While radiant with a mimic flame
Outside the sparkling drift became,
And through the bare-boughed lilac-tree
Our own warm hearth seemed blazing free.
The crane and pendent trammels showed,
The Turks' heads on the andirons glowed;
While childish fancy, prompt to tell
The meaning of the miracle,
Whispered the old rhyme: *"Under the tree,*
When fire outdoors burns merrily,
There the witches are making tea."

The moon above the eastern wood
Shone as its full; the hill-range stood
Transfigured in the silver flood,
Its blown snows flashing cold and keen,
Dead white, save where some sharp ravine
Took shadow, or the sombre green
Of hemlocks turned to pitchy black
Against the whiteness at their back.
For such a world and such a night
Most fitting that unwarming light,
Which only seemed where'er it fell
To make the coldness visible.

Shut in from all the world without,
We sat the clean-winged hearth about,
Content to let the north-wind roar
In baffled rage at pane and door,
While the red logs before us beat
The frost-line back with tropic heat;
And ever, when a louder blast
Shook beam and rafter as it passed,
The merrier up its roaring draught
The great throat of the chimney laughed.
The house-dog on his paws outspread
Laid to the fire his drowsy head,
The cat's dark silhouette on the wall
A couchant tiger's seemed to fall;
And, for the winter fireside meet,
Between the andirons' straddling feet,
The mug of cider simmered slow,
The apples sputtered in a row,
And, close at hand, the basket stood
With nuts from brown October's wood.

What matter how the night behaved?
What matter how the north-wind raved?
Blow high, blow low, not all its snow
Could quench our hearth-fire's ruddy glow.
O Time and Change!—with hair as gray
As was my sire's that winter day,
How strange it seems, with so much gone
Of life and love, to still live on!
Ah, brother! only I and thou
Are left of all that circle now,—

The dear home faces whereupon
That fitful firelight paled and shone.
Henceforward, listen as we will,
The voices of that hearth are still;
Look where we may, the wide earth o'er,
Those lighted faces smile no more.
We tread the paths their feet have worn,
    We sit beneath their orchard-trees,
    We hear, like them, the hum of bees
And rustle of the bladed corn;
We turn the pages that they read,
    Their written words we linger o'er,
But in the sun they cast no shade,
No voice is heard, no sign is made,
    No step is on the conscious floor!
Yet Love will dream, and Faith will trust,
(Since He who knows our need is just,)
That somehow, somewhere, meet we must.
Alas for him who never sees
The stars shine through his cypress-trees!
Who, hopeless, lays his dead away,
Nor looks to see the breaking day
Across the mournful marbles play!
Who hath not learned, in hours of faith,
    The truth to flesh and sense unknown,
That Life is ever lord of Death,
    And Love can never lose its own!

We sped the time with stories old,
Wrought puzzles out, and riddles told,
Or stammered from our school-book lore

"The Chief of Gambia's golden shore."
How often since, when all the land
Was clay in Slavery's shaping hand,
As if a trumpet called, I've heard
Dame Mercy Warren's rousing word:
"Does not the voice of reason cry,
    Claim the first right which Nature gave,
From the red scourge of bondage fly,
    Nor deign to live a burdened slave!"
Our father rode again his ride
On Memphremagog's wooded side;
Sat down again to moose and samp
In trapper's hut and Indian camp;
Lived o'er the old idyllic ease
Beneath St. François' hemlock-trees;
Again for him the moonlight shone
On Norman cap and bodiced zone;
Again he heard the violin play
Which led the village dance away,
And mingled in its merry whirl
The grandam and the laughing girl.
Or, nearer home, our steps he led
Where Salisbury's level marshes spread
    Mile-wide as flies the laden bee;
Where merry mowers, hale and strong,
Swept, scythe on scythe, their swaths along
    The low green prairies of the sea.
We shared the fishing off Boar's Head,
    And round the rocky Isles of Shoals
    The hake-broil on the drift-wood coals;
The chowder on the sand-beach made,

Dipped by the hungry, steaming hot,
With spoons of clam-shell from the pot.
We heard the tales of witchcraft old,
And dream and sign and marvel told
To sleepy listeners as they lay
Stretched idly on the salted hay,
Adrift along the winding shores,
When favoring breezes deigned to blow
The square sail of the gundalow
And idle lay the useless oars.
Our mother, while she turned her wheel
Or run the new-knit stocking-heel,
Told how the Indian hordes came down
At midnight on Cochecho town,
And how her own great-uncle bore
His cruel scalp-mark to fourscore.
Recalling, in her fitting phrase,
   So rich and picturesque and free,
   (The common unrhymed poetry
Of simple life and country ways,)
The story of her early days,—
She made us welcome to her home;
Old hearths grew wide to give us room;
We stole with her a frightened look
At the gray wizard's conjuring-book,
The fame whereof went far and wide
Through all the simple country side;
We heard the hawks at twilight play,
The boat-horn on Piscataqua,
The loon's weird laughter far away;
We fished her little trout-brook, knew

What flowers in wood and meadow grew,
What sunny hillsides autumn-brown
She climbed to shake the ripe nuts down,
Saw where in sheltered cove and bay
The ducks' black squadron anchored lay,
And heard the wild-geese calling loud
Beneath the gray November cloud.

Then, haply, with a look more grave,
And soberer tone, some tale she gave
From painful Sewell's ancient tome,
Beloved in every Quaker home,
Of faith fire-winged by martyrdom,
Or Chalkley's Journal, old and quaint,—
Gentlest of skippers, rare sea-saint!—
Who, when the dreary calms prevailed,
And water-butt and bread-cask failed,
And cruel, hungry eyes pursued
His portly presence mad for food,
With dark hints muttered under breath
Of casting lots for life or death,
Offered, if Heaven withheld supplies,
To be himself the sacrifice.
Then, suddenly, as if to save
The good man from his living grave,
A ripple on the water grew,
A school of porpoise flashed in view.
"Take, eat," he said, "and be content;
These fishes in my stead are sent
By Him who gave the tangled ram
To spare the child of Abraham."

Our uncle, innocent of books,
Was rich in lore of fields and brooks,
The ancient teachers never dumb
Of Nature's unhoused lyceum.
In moons and tides and weather wise,
He read the clouds as prophecies,
And foul or fair could well divine,
By many an occult hint and sign,
Holding the cunning-warded keys
To all the woodcraft mysteries;
Himself to Nature's heart so near
That all her voices in his ear
Of beast or bird had meanings clear,
Like Apollonius of old,
Who knew the tales the sparrows told,
Or Hermes, who interpreted
What the sage cranes of Nilus said;
A simple, guileless, childlike man,
Content to live where life began;
Strong only on his native grounds,
The little world of sights and sounds
Whose girdle was the parish bounds,
Whereof his fondly partial pride
The common features magnified,
As Surrey hills to mountains grew
In White of Selborne's loving view,—
He told how teal and loon he shot,
And how the eagle's eggs he got,
The feats on pond and river done,
The prodigies of rod and gun;
Till, warming with the tales he told,

Forgotten was the outside cold,
The bitter wind unheeded blew,
From ripening corn the pigeons flew,
The partridge drummed i' the wood, the mink
Went fishing down the river-brink.
In fields with bean or clover gay,
The woodchuck, like a hermit gray,
Peered from the doorway of his cell;
The muskrat plied the mason's trade,
And tier by tier his mud-walls laid;
And from the shagbark overhead
The grizzled squirrel dropped his shell.

Next, the dear aunt, whose smile of cheer
And voice in dreams I see and hear,—
The sweetest woman ever Fate
Perverse denied a household mate,
Who, lonely, homeless, not the less
Found peace in love's unselfishness,
And welcome wheresoe'er she went,
A calm and gracious element,
Whose presence seemed the sweet income
And womanly atmosphere of home,—
Called up her girlhood memories,
The huskings and the apple-bees,
The sleigh-rides and the summer sails,
Weaving through all the poor details
And homespun warp of circumstance
A golden woof-thread of romance.
For well she kept her genial mood
And simple faith of maidenhood;

Before her still a cloud-land lay,
The mirage loomed across her way;
The morning dew, that dries so soon
With others, glistened at her noon;
Through years of toil and soil and care
From glossy tress to thin gray hair,
All unprofaned she held apart
The virgin fancies of the heart.
Be shame to him of woman born
Who hath for such but thought of scorn.

There, too, our elder sister plied
Her evening task the stand beside;
A full, rich nature, free to trust,
Truthful and almost sternly just,
Impulsive, earnest, prompt to act,
And make her generous thought a fact,
Keeping with many a light disguise
The secret of self-sacrifice.
O heart sore-tried! thou hast the best
That Heaven itself could give thee,—rest,
Rest from all bitter thoughts and things!
　How many a poor one's blessing went
　With thee beneath the low green tent
Whose curtain never outward swings!

As one who held herself a part
Of all she saw, and let her heart
　Against the household bosom lean,
Upon the motley-braided mat
Our youngest and our dearest sat,

Lifting her large, sweet, asking eyes,
    Now bathed within the fadeless green
And holy peace of Paradise.
O, looking from some heavenly hill,
    Or from the shade of saintly palms,
    Or silver reach of river calms,
Do those large eyes behold me still?
With me one little year ago:—
The chill weight of the winter snow
    For months upon her grave has lain;
And now, when summer south-winds blow
    And brier and harebell bloom again,
I tread the pleasant paths we trod,
I see the violet-sprinkled sod
Whereon she leaned, too frail and weak
The hillside flowers she loved to seek,
Yet following me where'er I went
With dark eyes full of love's content.
The birds are glad; the brier-rose fills
The air with sweetness; all the hills
Stretch green to June's unclouded sky;
But still I wait with ear and eye
For something gone which should be nigh,
A loss in all familiar things,
In flower that blooms, and bird that sings.
And yet, dear heart! remembering thee,
    Am I not richer than of old?
Safe in thy immortality,
    What change can reach the wealth I hold?
    What chance can mar the pearl and gold
Thy love hath left in trust with me?

And while in life's late afternoon,
    Where cool and long the shadows grow,
I walk to meet the night that soon
    Shall shape and shadow overflow,
I cannot feel that thou art far,
Since near at need the angels are;
And when the sunset gates unbar,
    Shall I not see thee waiting stand,
And, white against the evening star,
    The welcome of thy beckoning hand?

Brisk wielder of the birch and rule,
The master of the district school
Held at the fire his favored place,
Its warm glow lit a laughing face
Fresh-hued and fair, where scarce appeared
The uncertain prophecy of beard.
He teased the mitten-blinded cat,
Played cross-pins on my uncle's hat,
Sang songs, and told us what befalls
In classic Dartmouth's college halls.
Born the wild Northern hills among,
From whence his yeoman father wrung
By patient toil subsistence scant,
Not competence and yet not want,
He early gained the power to pay
His cheerful, self-reliant way;
Could doff at ease his scholar's gown
To peddle wares from town to town;
Or through the long vacation's reach
In lonely lowland districts teach,

Where all the droll experience found
At stranger hearths in boarding round,
The moonlit skater's keen delight,
The sleigh-drive through the frosty night,
The rustic party, with its rough
Accompaniment of blind-man's-buff,
And whirling plate, and forfeits paid,
His winter task a pastime made.
Happy the snow-locked homes wherein
He tuned his merry violin,
Or played the athlete in the barn,
Or held the good dame's winding yarn,
Or mirth-provoking versions told
Of classic legends rare and old,
Wherein the scenes of Greece and Rome
Had all the commonplace of home,
And little seemed at best the odds
'Twixt Yankee pedlers and old gods;
Where Pindus-born Araxes took
The guise of any grist-mill brook,
And dread Olympus at his will
Became a huckleberry hill.

A careless boy that night he seemed;
  But at his desk he had the look
And air of one who wisely schemed,
  And hostage from the future took
  In trainéd thought and lore of book.
Large-brained, clear-eyed,—of such as he
Shall Freedom's young apostles be,
Who, following in War's bloody trail,

Shall every lingering wrong assail;
All chains from limb and spirit strike,
Uplift the black and white alike;
Scatter before their swift advance
The darkness and the ignorance,
The pride, the lust, the squalid sloth,
Which nurtured Treason's monstrous growth,
Made murder pastime, and the hell
Of prison-torture possible;
The cruel lie of caste refute,
Old forms remould, and substitute
For Slavery's lash and freeman's will,
For blind routine, wise-handed skill;
A school-house plant on every hill,
Stretching in radiate nerve-lines thence
The quick wires of intelligence;
Till North and South together brought
Shall own the same electric thought,
In peace a common flag salute,
And, side by side in labor's free
And unresentful rivalry,
Harvest the fields wherein they fought.

Another guest that winter night
Flashed back from lustrous eyes the light.
Unmarked by time, and yet not young,
The honeyed music of her tongue
And words of meekness scarcely told
A nature passionate and bold,
Strong, self-concentred, spurning guide,
Its milder features dwarfed beside

Her unbent will's majestic pride.
She sat among us, at the best,
A not unfeared, half-welcome guest,
Rebuking with her cultured phrase
Our homeliness of words and ways.
A certain pard-like, treacherous grace
    Swayed the lithe limbs and drooped the lash,
    Lent the white teeth their dazzling flash;
    And under low brows, black with night,
    Rayed out at times a dangerous light;
The sharp heat-lightnings of her face
Presaging ill to him whom Fate
Condemned to share her love or hate.
A woman tropical, intense
In thought and act, in soul and sense,
She blended in a like degree
The vixen and the devotee,
Revealing with each freak or feint
    The temper of Petruchio's Kate,
The raptures of Siena's saint.
Her tapering hand and rounded wrist
Had facile power to form a fist;
The warm, dark languish of her eyes
Was never safe from wrath's surprise.
Brows saintly calm and lips devout
Knew every change of scowl and pout;
And the sweet voice had notes more high
And shrill for social battle-cry.

Since then what old cathedral town
Has missed her pilgrim staff and gown,

What convent-gate has held its lock
Against the challenge of her knock!
Through Smyrna's plague-hushed thoroughfares,
Up sea-set Malta's rocky stairs,
Gray olive slopes of hills that hem
Thy tombs and shrines, Jerusalem,
Or startling on her desert throne
The crazy Queen of Lebanon
With claims fantastic as her own,
Her tireless feet have held their way;
And still, unrestful, bowed, and gray,
She watches under Eastern skies,
    With hope each day renewed and fresh,
    The Lord's quick coming in the flesh,
Whereof she dreams and prophesies!

Where'er her troubled path may be,
    The Lord's sweet pity with her go!
The outward wayward life we see,
    The hidden springs we may not know.
Nor is it given us to discern
    What threads the fatal sisters spun,
    Through what ancestral years has run
The sorrow with the woman born,
What forged her cruel chain of moods,
What set her feet in solitudes,
    And held the love within her mute,
What mingled madness in the blood,
    A life-long discord and annoy,
    Water of tears with oil of joy,
And hid within the folded bud
    Perversities of flower and fruit.

It is not ours to separate
The tangled skein of will and fate,
To show what metes and bounds should stand
Upon the soul's debatable land,
And between choice and Providence
Divide the circle of events;
But He who knows our frame is just,
    Merciful, and compassionate,
And full of sweet assurances
And hope for all the language is,
That He remembereth we are dust!

At last the great logs, crumbling low,
Sent out a dull and duller glow,
The bull's-eye watch that hung in view,
Ticking its weary circuit through,
Pointed with mutely-warning sign
Its black hand to the hour of nine.
That sign the pleasant circle broke:
My uncle ceased his pipe to smoke,
Knocked from its bowl the refuse gray
And laid it tenderly away,
Then roused himself to safely cover
The dull red brands with ashes over.
And while, with care, our mother laid
The work aside, her steps she stayed
One moment, seeking to express
Her grateful sense of happiness
For food and shelter, warmth and health,
And love's contentment more than wealth,
With simple wishes (not the weak,

Vain prayers which no fulfilment seek,
But such as warm the generous heart,
O'er-prompt to do with Heaven its part)
That none might lack, that bitter night,
For bread and clothing, warmth and light.

Within our beds awhile we heard
The wind that round the gables roared,
With now and then a ruder shock,
Which made our very bedsteads rock.
We heard the loosened clapboards tost,
The board-nails snapping in the frost;
And on us, through the unplastered wall,
Felt the light sifted snow-flakes fall.
But sleep stole on, as sleep will do
When hearts are light and life is new;
Faint and more faint the murmurs grew,
Till in the summer-land of dreams
They softened to the sound of streams,
Low stir of leaves, and dip of oars,
And lapsing waves on quiet shores.

Next morn we wakened with the shout
Of merry voices high and clear;
And saw the teamsters drawing near
To break the drifted highways out.
Down the long hillside treading slow
We saw the half-buried oxen go,
Shaking the snow from heads uptost,
Their straining nostrils white with frost.
Before our door the straggling train

Drew up, an added team to gain.
The elders threshed their hands a-cold,
    Passed, with the cider-mug, their jokes
    From lip to lip; the younger folks
Down the loose snow-banks, wrestling, rolled,
Then toiled again the cavalcade
    O'er windy hill, through clogged ravine,
    And woodland paths that wound between
Low drooping pine-boughs winter-weighed.
From every barn a team afoot,
At every house a new recruit,
Where, drawn by Nature's subtlest law,
Haply the watchful young men saw
Sweet doorway pictures of the curls
And curious eyes of merry girls,
Lifting their hands in mock defence
Against the snow-ball's compliments,
And reading in each missive tost
The charm with Eden never lost.

We heard once more the sleigh-bells' sound;
    And, following where the teamsters led,
The wise old Doctor went his round,
Just pausing at our door to say,
In the brief autocratic way
Of one who, prompt at Duty's call,
Was free to urge her claim on all,
    That some poor neighbor sick abed
At night our mother's aid would need.
For, one in generous thought and deed,
    What mattered in the sufferer's sight
    The Quaker matron's inward light,

The Doctor's mail of Calvin's creed?
All hearts confess the saints elect
   Who, twain in faith, in love agree,
And melt not in an acid sect
   The Christian pearl of charity!

So days went on: a week had passed
Since the great world was heard from last.
The Almanac we studied o'er,
Read and reread our little store,
Of books and pamphlets, scarce a score;
One harmless novel, mostly hid
From younger eyes, a book forbid,
And poetry, (or good or bad,
A single book was all we had,)
Where Ellwood's meek, drab-skirted Muse,
   A stranger to the heathen Nine,
   Sang, with a somewhat nasal whine,
The wars of David and the Jews.
At last the floundering carrier bore
The village paper to our door.
Lo! broadening outward as we read,
To warmer zones the horizon spread;
In panoramic length unrolled
We saw the marvels that it told.
Before us passed the painted Creeks,
   And daft McGregor on his raids
   In Costa Rica's everglades.
And up Taygetos winding slow
Rode Ypsilanti's Mainote Greeks,
A Turk's head at each saddle-bow!

Welcome to us its week-old news,
Its corner for the rustic Muse,
    Its monthly gauge of snow and rain,
Its record, mingling in a breath
The wedding bell and dirge of death;
Jest, anecdote, and love-lorn tale,
The latest culprit sent to jail;
Its hue and cry of stolen and lost,
Its vendue sales and goods at cost,
    And traffic calling loud for gain.
We felt the stir of hall and street,
The pulse of life that round us beat;
The chill embargo of the snow
Was melted in the genial glow;
Wide swung again our ice-locked door,
And all the world was ours once more!

Clasp, Angel of the backward look
    And folded wings of ashen gray
    And voice of echoes far away,
The brazen covers of thy book;
The weird palimpsest old and vast,
Wherein thou hid'st the spectral past;
Where, closely mingling, pale and glow
The characters of joy and woe;
The monographs of outlived years,
Or smile-illumed or dim with tears,
    Green hills of life that slope to death,
And haunts of home, whose vistaed trees
Shade off to mournful cypresses
    With the white amaranths underneath.

Even while I look, I can but heed
    The restless sands' incessant fall,
Importunate hours that hours succeed,
Each clamorous with its own sharp need,
    And duty keeping pace with all.
Shut down and clasp the heavy lids;
I hear again the voice that bids
The dreamer leave his dream midway
For larger hopes and graver fears:
Life greatens in these later years,
The century's aloe flowers to-day!

Yet, haply, in some lull of life,
Some Truce of God which breaks its strife,
The worldling's eyes shall gather dew,
    Dreaming in throngful city ways
Of winter joys his boyhood knew;
And dear and early friends—the few
Who yet remain—shall pause to view
    These Flemish pictures of old days;
Sit with me by the homestead hearth,
And stretch the hands of memory forth
    To warm them at the wood-fire's blaze!
And thanks untraced to lips unknown
Shall greet me like the odors blown
From unseen meadows newly mown,
Or lilies floating in some pond,
Wood-fringed, the wayside gaze beyond;
The traveller owns the grateful sense
Of sweetness near, he knows not whence,
And, pausing, takes with forehead bare
The benediction of the air.

Abraham Davenport

In the old days (a custom laid aside
With breeches and cocked hats) the people sent
Their wisest men to make the public laws.
And so, from a brown homestead, where the Sound
Drinks the small tribute of the Mianas,
Waved over by the woods of Rippowams,
And hallowed by pure lives and tranquil deaths,
Stamford sent up to the councils of the State
Wisdom and grace in Abraham Davenport.

'T was on a May-day of the far old year
Seventeen hundred eighty, that there fell
Over the bloom and sweet life of the Spring,
Over the fresh earth and the heaven of noon,
A horror of great darkness, like the night
In day of which the Norland sagas tell,—
The Twilight of the Gods. The low-hung sky
Was black with ominous clouds, save where its rim
Was fringed with a dull glow, like that which climbs
The crater's sides from the red hell below.
Birds ceased to sing, and all the barn-yard fowls
Roosted; the cattle at the pasture bars
Lowed, and looked homeward; bats on leathern wings
Flitted abroad; the sounds of labor died;
Men prayed, and women wept; all ears grew sharp
To hear the doom-blast of the trumpet shatter
The black sky, that the dreadful face of Christ
Might look from the rent clouds, not as he looked

A loving guest at Bethany, but stern
As Justice and inexorable Law.

   Meanwhile in the old State-House, dim as ghosts,
Sat the lawgivers of Connecticut,
Trembling beneath their legislative robes.
"It is the Lord's Great Day! Let us adjourn,"
Some said; and then, as if with one accord,
All eyes were turned to Abraham Davenport.
He rose, slow cleaving with his steady voice
The intolerable hush. "This well may be
The Day of Judgment which the world awaits;
But be it so or not, I only know
My present duty, and my Lord's command
To occupy till he come. So at the post
Where he hath set me in his providence,
I choose, for one, to meet him face to face,—
No faithless servant frightened from my task,
But ready when the Lord of the harvest calls;
And therefore, with all reverence, I would say,
Let God do his work, we will see to ours.
Bring in the candles." And they brought them in.

   Then by the flaring lights the Speaker read,
Albeit with husky voice and shaking hands,
An act to amend an act to regulate
The shad and alewive fisheries. Whereupon
Wisely and well spake Abraham Davenport,
Straight to the question, with no figures of speech
Save the ten Arab signs, yet not without
The shrewd dry humor natural to the man:

His awe-struck colleagues listening all the while,
Between the pauses of his argument,
To hear the thunder of the wrath of God
Break from the hollow trumpet of the cloud.

    And there he stands in memory to this day,
Erect, self-poised, a rugged face, half seen
Against the background of unnatural dark,
A witness to the ages as they pass,
That simple duty hath no place for fear.

———

The harp at Nature's advent strung
    Has never ceased to play;
The song the stars of morning sung
    Has never died away.

And prayer is made, and praise is given,
    By all things near and far:
The ocean looketh up to heaven,
    And mirrors every star.

Its waves are kneeling on the strand,
    As kneels the human knee,
Their white locks bowing to the sand,
    The priesthood of the sea!

They pour their glittering treasures forth,
    Their gifts of pearl they bring,
And all the listening hills of earth
    Take up the song they sing.

The green earth sends her incense up
  From many a mountain shrine;
From folded leaf and dewy cup
  She pours her sacred wine.

The mists above the morning rills
  Rise white as wings of prayer;
The altar curtains of the hills
  Are sunset's purple air.

The winds with hymns of praise are loud,
  Or low with sobs of pain,—
The thunder-organ of the cloud,
  The dropping tears of rain.

With drooping head and branches crossed
  The twilight forest grieves,
Or speaks with tongues of Pentecost
  From all its sunlit leaves.

The blue sky is the temple's arch,
  Its transept earth and air,
The music of its starry march
  The chorus of a prayer.

So Nature keeps the reverent frame
  With which her years began,
And all her signs and voices shame
  The prayerless heart of man.

Prelude

Along the roadside, like the flowers of gold
That tawny Incas for their gardens wrought,
Heavy with sunshine droops the golden-rod,
And the red pennons of the cardinal-flowers
Hang motionless upon their upright staves.
The sky is hot and hazy, and the wind,
Wing-weary with its long flight from the south,
Unfelt; yet, closely scanned, yon maple leaf
With faintest motion, as one stirs in dreams,
Confesses it. The locust by the wall
Stabs the noon-silence with his sharp alarm.
A single hay-cart down the dusty road
Creaks slowly, with its driver fast asleep
On the load's top. Against the neighboring hill,
Huddled along the stone wall's shady side,
The sheep show white, as if a snow-drift still
Defied the dog-star. Through the open door
A drowsy smell of flowers—gray heliotrope,
And white sweet-clover, and shy mignonette—
Comes faintly in, and silent chorus lends
To the pervading symphony of peace.

No time is this for hands long overworn
To task their strength; and (unto Him be praise
Who giveth quietness!) the stress and strain
Of years that did the work of centuries
Have ceased, and we can draw our breath once more
Freely and full. So, as yon harvesters

Make glad their nooning underneath the elms
With tale and riddle and old snatch of song,
I lay aside grave themes, and idly turn
The leaves of Memory's sketch-book, dreaming o'er
Old summer pictures of the quiet hills,
And human life, as quiet, at their feet.

And yet not idly all. A farmer's son,
Proud of field-lore and harvest craft, and feeling
All their fine possibilities, how rich
And restful even poverty and toil
Become when beauty, harmony, and love
Sit at their humble hearth as angels sat
At evening in the patriarch's tent, when man
Makes labor noble, and his farmer's frock
The symbol of a Christian chivalry
Tender and just and generous to her
Who clothes with grace all duty; still, I know
Too well the picture has another side,—
How wearily the grind of toil goes on
Where love is wanting, how the eye and ear
And heart are starved amidst the plentitude
Of nature, and how hard and colorless
Is life without an atmosphere. I look
Across the lapse of half a century,
And call to mind old homesteads, where no flower
Told that the spring had come, but evil weeds,
Nightshade and rough-leaved burdock in the place
Of the sweet doorway greeting of the rose
And honeysuckle, where the house walls seemed
Blistering in sun, without a tree or vine

To cast the tremulous shadow of its leaves
Across the curtainless windows from whose panes
Fluttered the signal rags of shiftlessness;
Within, the cluttered kitchen-floor, unwashed
(Broom-clean I think they called it); the best room
Stifling with cellar damp, shut from the air
In hot midsummer, bookless, pictureless
Save the inevitable sampler hung
Over the fireplace, or a mourning-piece,
A green-haired woman, peony-cheeked, beneath
Impossible willows; the wide-throated hearth
Bristling with faded pine-boughs half concealing
The piled-up rubbish at the chimney's back;
And, in sad keeping with all things about them,
Shrill, querulous women, sour and sullen men,
Untidy, loveless, old before their time,
With scarce a human interest save their own
Monotonous round of small economies,
Or the poor scandal of the neighborhood;
Blind to the beauty everywhere revealed,
Treading the May-flowers with regardless feet;
For them the song-sparrow and the bobolink
Sang not, nor winds made music in the leaves;
For them in vain October's holocaust
Burned, gold and crimson, over all the hills,
The sacramental mystery of the woods.
Church-goers, fearful of the unseen Powers,
But grumbling over pulpit-tax and pew-rent,
Saving, as shrewd economists, their souls
And winter pork with the least possible outlay
Of salt and sanctity; in daily life

Showing as little actual comprehension
Of Christian charity and love and duty,
As if the Sermon on the Mount had been
Outdated like a last year's almanac:
Rich in broad woodlands and in half-tilled fields,
And yet so pinched and bare and comfortless,
The veriest straggler limping on his rounds,
The sun and air his sole inheritance,
Laughed at a poverty that paid its taxes,
And hugged his rags in self-complacency!

Not such should be the homesteads of a land
Where whoso wisely wills and acts may dwell
As king and lawgiver, in broad-acred state,
With beauty, art, taste, culture, books, to make
His hour of leisure richer than a life
Of fourscore to the barons of old time,
Our yeoman should be equal to his home
Set in the fair, green valleys, purple walled,
A man to match his mountains, not to creep
Dwarfed and abased below them. I would fain
In this light way (of which I needs must own
With the knife-grinder of whom Canning sings,
"Story, God bless you! I have none to tell you!")
Invite the eye to see and heart to feel
The beauty and the joy within their reach,—
Home, and home loves, and the beatitudes
Of nature free to all. Haply in years
That wait to take the places of our own,
Heard where some breezy balcony looks down
On happy homes, or where the lake in the moon

Sleeps dreaming of the mountains, fair as Ruth,
In the old Hebrew pastoral, at the feet
Of Boaz, even this simple lay of mine
May seem the burden of a prophecy,
Finding its late fulfilment in a change
Slow as the oak's growth, lifting manhood up
Through broader culture, finer manners, love,
And reverence, to the level of the hills.

O Golden Age, whose light is of the dawn,
And not of sunset, forward, not behind,
Flood the new heavens and earth, and with thee bring
All the old virtues, whatsoever things
Are pure and honest and of good repute,
But add thereto whatever bard has sung
Or seer has told of when in trance and dream
They saw the Happy Isles of prophecy!
Let Justice hold her scale, and Truth divide
Between the right and wrong; but give the heart
The freedom of its fair inheritance;
Let the poor prisoner, cramped and starved so long,
At Nature's table feast his ear and eye
With joy and wonder; let all harmonies
Of sound, form, color, motion, wait upon
The princely guest, whether in soft attire
Of leisure clad, or the coarse frock of toil.
And, lending life to the dead form of faith,
Give human nature reverence for the sake
Of One who bore it, making it divine
With the ineffable tenderness of God;
Let common need, the brotherhood of prayer,

The heirship of an unknown destiny,
The unsolved mystery round about us, make
A man more precious than the gold of Ophir.
Sacred, inviolate, unto whom all things
Should minister, as outward types and signs
Of the eternal beauty which fulfils
The one great purpose of creation, Love,
The sole necessity of Earth and Heaven!

The Hive at Gettysburg

In the old Hebrew myth the lion's frame,
   So terrible alive,
Bleached by the desert's sun and wind, became
   The wandering wild bees' hive;
And he who, lone and naked-handed, tore
   Those jaws of death apart,
In after time drew forth their honeyed store
   To strengthen his strong heart.

Dead seemed the legend: but it only slept
   To wake beneath our sky;
Just on the spot whence ravening Treason crept
   Back to its lair to die,
Bleeding and torn from Freedom's mountain bounds,
   A stained and shattered drum
Is now the hive where, on their flowery rounds,
   The wild bees go and come.

Unchallenged by a ghostly sentinel,
    They wander wide and far,
Along green hillsides, sown with shot and shell,
    Through vales once choked with war.
The low reveille of their battle-drum
    Disturbs no morning prayer;
With deeper peace in summer noons their hum
    Fills all the drowsy air.

And Samson's riddle is our own to-day,
    Of sweetness from the strong,
Of union, peace, and freedom plucked away
    From the rent jaws of wrong.
From Treason's death we draw a purer life,
    As, from the beast he slew,
A sweetness sweeter for his bitter strife
    The old-time athlete drew!

In School-Days

Still sits the school-house by the road,
    A ragged beggar sunning;
Around it still the sumachs grow,
    And blackberry vines are running.

Within, the master's desk is seen,
    Deep scarred by raps official;
The warping floor, the battered seats,
    The jack-knife's carved initial;

The charcoal frescos on its wall;
   Its door's worn sill, betraying
The feet that, creeping slow to school,
   Went storming out to playing!

Long years ago a winter sun
   Shone over it at setting;
Lit up its western window-panes,
   And low eaves' icy fretting.

It touched the tangled golden curls,
   And brown eyes full of grieving,
Of one who still her steps delayed
   When all the school were leaving.

For near her stood the little boy
   Her childish favor singled;
His cap pulled low upon a face
   Where pride and shame were mingled.

Pushing with restless feet the snow
   To right and left, he lingered;—
As restlessly her tiny hands
   The blue-checked apron fingered.

He saw her lift her eyes; he felt
   The soft hand's light caressing,
And heard the tremble of her voice,
   As if a fault confessing.

"I'm sorry that I spelt the word:
    I hate to go above you,
Because,"—the brown eyes lower fell,—
    "Because, you see, I love you!"

Still memory to a gray-haired man
    That sweet child-face is showing.
Dear girl! the grasses on her grave
    Have forty years been growing!

He lives to learn, in life's hard school,
    How few who pass above him
Lament their triumph and his loss,
    Like her,—because they love him.

The Brewing of Soma

*"These libations mixed with milk have been prepared for Indra:
offer Soma to the drinker of Soma."*
                    —*VASHISTA, Trans. by MAX MÜLLER.*

The fagots blazed, the caldron's smoke
    Up through the green wood curled;
"Bring honey from the hollow oak,
Bring milky sap," the brewers spoke,
    In the childhood of the world.

And brewed they well or brewed they ill,
    The priests thrust in their rods,
First tasted, and then drank their fill,
And shouted, with one voice and will,
    "Behold the drink of gods!"

They drank, and lo! in heart and brain
   A new, glad life began;
The gray of hair grew young again,
The sick man laughed away his pain,
   The cripple leaped and ran.

"Drink, mortals, what the gods have sent,
   Forget your long annoy."
So sang the priests. From tent to tent
The Soma's sacred madness went,
   A storm of drunken joy.

Then knew each rapt inebriate
   A winged and glorious birth,
Soared upward, with strange joy elate,
Beat, with dazed head, Varuna's gate,
   And, sobered, sank to earth.

The land with Soma's praises rang;
   On Gihon's banks of shade
Its hymns the dusky maidens sang;
In joy of life or mortal pang
   All men to Soma prayed.

The morning twilight of the race
   Sends down these matin psalms;
And still with wondering eyes we trace
The simple prayers to Soma's grace,
   That Vedic verse embalms.

As in that child-world's early year,
  Each after age has striven
By music, incense, vigils drear,
And trance, to bring the skies more near,
  Or lift men up to heaven!—

Some fever of the blood and brain,
  Some self-exalting spell,
The scourger's keen delight of pain,
The Dervish dance, the Orphic strain,
  The wild-haired Bacchant's yell,—

The desert's hair-grown hermit sunk
  The saner brute below;
The naked Santon, hashish-drunk,
The cloister madness of the monk,
  The fakir's torture-show!

And yet the past comes round again,
  And new doth old fulfil;
In sensual transports wild as vain
We brew in many a Christian fane
  The heathen Soma still!

Dear Lord and Father of mankind,
  Forgive our foolish ways!
Reclothe us in our rightful mind,
In purer lives thy service find,
  In deeper reverence, praise.

In simple trust like theirs who heard
    Beside the Syrian sea
The gracious calling of the Lord,
Let us, like them, without a word,
    Rise up and follow thee.

O Sabbath rest by Galilee!
    O calm of hills above,
Where Jesus knelt to share with thee
The silence of eternity
    Interpreted by love!

With that deep hush subduing all
    Our words and works that drown
The tender whisper of thy call,
As noiseless let thy blessing fall
    As fell thy manna down.

Drop thy still dews of quietness,
    Till all our strivings cease;
Take from our souls the strain and stress,
And let our ordered lives confess
    The beauty of thy peace.

Breathe through the heats of our desire
    Thy coolness and thy balm;
Let sense be dumb, let flesh retire;
Speak through the earthquake, wind, and fire,
    O still, small voice of calm!

The Pressed Gentian

The time of gifts has come again,
And, on my northern window-pane,
Outlined against the day's brief light,
A Christmas token hangs in sight.
The wayside travelers, as they pass,
Mark the gray disk of clouded glass;
And the dull blankness seems, perchance,
Folly to their wise ignorance.

They cannot from their outlook see
The perfect grace it hath for me;
For there the flower, whose fringes through
The frosty breath of autumn blew,
Turns from without its face of bloom
To the warm tropic of my room,
As fair as when beside its brook
The hue of bending skies it took.

So, from the trodden ways of earth,
Seem some sweet souls who veil their worth,
And offer to the careless glance
The clouding gray of circumstance.
They blossom best where hearth-fires burn,
To loving eyes alone they turn
The flowers of inward grace, that hide
Their beauty from the world outside.

But deeper meanings come to me,
My half-immortal flower, from thee!

Man judges from a partial view,
None ever yet his brother knew;
The Eternal Eye that sees the whole
May better read the darkened soul,
And find, to outward sense denied,
The flower upon its inmost side!

The Witch of Wenham

I

Along Crane River's sunny slopes
    Blew warm the winds of May,
And over Naumkeag's ancient oaks
    The green outgrew the gray.

The grass was green on Rial-side,
    The early birds at will
Waked up the violet in its dell,
    The wind-flower on its hill.

"Where go you, in your Sunday coat?
    Son Andrew, tell me, pray."
"For strip èd perch in Wenham Lake
    I go to fish to-day."

"Unharmed of thee in Wenham Lake
    The mottled perch shall be:
A blue-eyed witch sits on the bank
    And weaves her net for thee.

"She weaves her golden hair; she sings
    Her spell-song low and faint;
The wickedest witch in Salem jail
    Is to that girl a saint."

"Nay, mother, hold thy cruel tongue;
    God knows," the young man cried,
"He never made a whiter soul
    Than hers by Wenham side.

"She tends her mother sick and blind,
    And every want supplies;
To her above the blessed Book
    She lends her soft blue eyes.

"Her voice is glad with holy songs,
    Her lips are sweet with prayer;
Go where you will, in ten miles round
    Is none more good and fair."

"Son Andrew, for the love of God
    And of thy mother, stay!"
She clasped her hands, she wept aloud,
    But Andrew rode away.

"O reverend sir, my Andrew's soul
    The Wenham witch has caught;
She holds him with the curlèd gold
    Whereof her snare is wrought.

"She charms him with her great blue eyes,
　　She binds him with her hair;
Oh, break the spell with holy words,
　　Unbind him with a prayer!"

"Take heart," the painful preacher said,
　　"This mischief shall not be;
The witch shall perish in her sins
　　And Andrew shall go free.

"Our poor Ann Putnam testifies
　　She saw her weave a spell,
Bare-armed, loose-haired, at full of moon,
　　Around a dried-up well.

"'Spring up, O well!' she softly sang
　　The Hebrew's old refrain
(For Satan uses Bible words),
　　Till water flowed amain.

"And many a goodwife heard her speak
　　By Wenham water words
That made the buttercups take wings
　　And turn to yellow birds.

"They say that swarming wild bees seek
　　The hive at her command;
And fishes swim to take their food
　　From out her dainty hand.

"Meek as she sits in meeting-time,
    The godly minister
Notes well the spell that doth compel
    The young men's eyes to her.

"The mole upon her dimpled chin
    Is Satan's seal and sign;
Her lips are red with evil bread
    And stain of unblest wine.

"For Tituba, my Indian, saith
    At Quasycung she took
The Black Man's godless sacrament
    And signed his dreadful book.

"Last night my sore-afflicted child
    Against the young witch cried.
To take her Marshal Herrick rides
    Even now to Wenham side."

The marshal in his saddle sat,
    His daughter at his knee;
"I go to fetch that arrant witch,
    Thy fair playmate," quoth he.

"Her spectre walks the parsonage,
    And haunts both hall and stair;
They know her by the great blues eyes
    And floating gold of hair."

"They lie, they lie, my father dear!
    No foul old witch is she,
But sweet and good and crystal-pure
    As Wenham waters be."

"I tell thee, child, the Lord hath set
    Before us good and ill,
And woe to all whose carnal loves
    Oppose his righteous will.

"Between Him and the powers of hell
    Choose thou, my child, to-day:
No sparing hand, no pitying eye,
    When God commands to slay!"

He went his way; the old wives shook
    With fear as he drew nigh;
The children in the dooryards held
    Their breath as he passed by.

Too well they knew the gaunt gray horse
    The grim witch-hunter rode—
The pale Apocalyptic beast
    By grisly Death bestrode.

II

Oh, fair the face of Wenham Lake
    Upon the young girl's shone,
Her tender mouth, her dreaming eyes,
    Her yellow hair outblown.

By happy youth and love attuned
  To natural harmonies,
The singing birds, the whispering wind,
  She sat beneath the trees.

Sat shaping for her bridal dress
  Her mother's wedding gown,
When lo! the marshal, writ in hand,
  From Alford hill rode down.

His face was hard with cruel fear,
  He grasped the maiden's hands:
"Come with me unto Salem town,
  For so the law commands!"

"Oh, let me to my mother say
  Farewell before I go!"
He closer tied her little hands
  Unto his saddle bow.

"Unhand me," cried she piteously,
  "For thy sweet daughter's sake."
"I'll keep my daughter safe," he said,
  "From the witch of Wenham Lake."

"Oh, leave me for my mother's sake,
  She needs my eyes to see."
"Those eyes, young witch, the crows shall peck
  From off the gallows-tree."

He bore her to a farm-house old
   And up its stairway long,
And closed on her the garret-door
   With iron bolted strong.

The day died out, the night came down.
   Her evening prayer she said,
While, through the dark, strange faces seemed
   To mock her as she prayed.

The present horror deepened all
   The fears her childhood knew;
The awe wherewith the air was filled
   With every breath she drew.

And could it be, she trembling asked,
   Some secret thought or sin
Had shut good angels from her heart
   And let the bad ones in?

Had she in some forgotten dream
   Let go her hold on Heaven,
And sold herself unwittingly
   To spirits unforgiven?

Oh, weird and still the dark hours passed;
   No human sound she heard,
But up and down the chimney stack
   The swallows moaned and stirred.

And o'er her, with a dread surmise
   Of evil sight and sound,
The blind bats on their leathern wings
   Went wheeling round and round.

Low hanging in the midnight sky
   Looked in a half-faced moon.
Was it a dream, or did she hear
   Her lover's whistled tune?

She forced the oaken scuttle back;
   A whisper reached her ear:
"Slide down the roof to me," it said,
   "So softly none may hear."

She slid along the sloping roof
   Till from its eaves she hung,
And felt the loosened shingles yield
   To which her fingers clung.

Below, her lover stretched his hands
   And touched her feet so small;
"Drop down to me, dear heart," he said,
   "My arms shall break the fall."

He set her on his pillion soft,
   Her arms about him twined;
And, noiseless as if velvet-shod,
   They left the house behind.

But when they reached the open way,
   Full free the rein he cast;
Oh, never through the mirk midnight
   Rode man and maid more fast.

Along the wild wood-paths they sped,
   The bridgeless streams they swam;
At set of moon they passed the Bass,
   At sunrise Agawam.

At high noon on the Merrimac
   The ancient ferryman
Forgot, at times, his idle oars,
   So fair a freight to scan.

And when from off his grounded boat
   He saw them mount and ride,
"God keep her from the evil eye,
   And harm of witch!" he cried.

The maiden laughed, as youth will laugh
   At all its fears gone by;
"He does not know," she whispered low,
   "A little witch am I."

All day he urged his weary horse,
   And, in the red sundown,
Drew rein before a friendly door
   In distant Berwick town.

A fellow-feeling for the wronged
    The Quaker people felt;
And safe beside their kindly hearths
    The hunted maiden dwelt,

Until from off its breast the land
    The haunting horror threw,
And hatred, born of ghastly dreams,
    To shame and pity grew.

Sad were the year's spring morns, and sad
    Its golden summer day,
But blithe and glad its withered fields,
    And skies of ashen gray;

For spell and charm had power no more,
    The spectres ceased to roam,
And scattered households knelt again
    Around the hearths of home.

And when once more by Beaver Dam
    The meadow-lark outsang,
And once again on all the hills
    The early violets sprang,

And all the windy pasture slopes
    Lay green within the arms
Of creeks that bore the salted sea
    To pleasant inland farms,

The smith filed off the chains he forged,
    The jail-bolts backward fell;
And youth and hoary age came forth
    Like souls escaped from hell.

The Henchman

My lady walks her morning round,
My lady's page her fleet greyhound,
My lady's hair the fond winds stir,
And all the birds make songs for her.

Her thrushes sing in Rathburn bowers,
And Rathburn side is gay with flowers;
But ne'er like hers, in flower or bird,
Was beauty seen or music heard.

The distance of the stars is hers;
The least of all her worshippers,
The dust beneath her dainty heel,
She knows not that I see or feel.

O proud and calm!—she cannot know
Where'er she goes with her I go;
O cold and fair!—she cannot guess
I kneel to share her hound's caress!

Gay knights beside her hunt and hawk,
I rob their ears of her sweet talk;
Her suitors come from east and west,
I steal her smiles from every guest.

Unheard of her, in loving words,
I greet her with the song of birds;
I reach her with her green-armed bowers,
I kiss her with the lips of flowers.

The hound and I are on her trail,
The wind and I uplift her veil;
As if the calm, cold moon she were,
And I the tide, I follow her.

As unrebuked as they, I share
The license of the sun and air,
And in a common homage hide
My worship from her scorn and pride.

World-wide apart, and yet so near,
I breathe her charmèd atmosphere,
Wherein to her my service brings
The reverence due to holy things.

Her maiden pride, her haughty name,
My dumb devotion shall not shame;
The love that no return doth crave
To knightly levels lifts the slave.

No lance have I, in joust or fight,
To splinter in my lady's sight;
But, at her feet, how blest were I
For any need of hers to die!

At Last

When on my day of life the night is falling,
   And, in the winds from unsunned spaces blown,
I hear far voices out of darkness calling
   My feet to paths unknown,

Thou who hast made my home of life so pleasant,
   Leave not its tenant when its walls decay;
O Love Divine, O Helper ever present,
   Be Thou my strength and stay!

Be near me when all else is from me drifting:
   Earth, sky, home's pictures, days of shade and shine,
And kindly faces to my own uplifting
   The love which answers mine.

I have but Thee, my Father! let Thy spirit
   Be with me then to comfort and uphold;
No gate of pearl, no branch of palm I merit,
   Nor street of shining gold.

Suffice it if—my good and ill unreckoned,
   And both forgiven through thy abounding grace—
I find myself by hands familiar beckoned
   Unto my fitting place.

Some humble door among Thy many mansions,
   Some sheltering shade where sin and striving cease,
And flows forever through heaven's green expansions
   The river of Thy peace.

There, from the music round about me stealing,
   I fain would learn the new and holy song,
And find at last, beneath Thy trees of healing,
   The life for which I long.

Sweet Fern

The subtle power in perfume found
   Nor priest nor sibyl vainly learned;
On Grecian shrine or Aztec mound
   No censer idly burned.

That power the old-time worships knew,
   The Corybantes' frenzied dance,
The Pythian priestess swooning through
   The wonderland of trance.

And Nature holds, in wood and field,
   Her thousand sunlit censers still;
To spells of flower and shrub we yield
   Against or with our will.

I climbed a hill path strange and new
   With slow feet, pausing at each turn;
A sudden waft of west wind blew
   The breath of the sweet fern.

That fragrance from my vision swept
   The alien landscape; in its stead,
Up fairer hills of youth I stepped,
   As light of heart as tread.

I saw my boyhood's lakelet shine
   Once more through rifts of woodland shade;
I knew my river's winding line
   By morning mist betrayed.

With me June's freshness, lapsing brook,
   Murmurs of leaf and bee, the call
Of birds, and one in voice and look
   In keeping with them all.

A fern beside the way we went
   She plucked, and, smiling, held it up,
While from her hand the wild, sweet scent
   I drank as from a cup.

O potent witchery of smell!
   The dust-dry leaves to life return,
And she who plucked them owns the spell
   And lifts her ghostly fern.

Or sense or spirit? Who shall say
   What touch the chord of memory thrills?
It passed, and left the August day
   Ablaze on lonely hills.

Burning Drift-Wood

Before my drift-wood fire I sit,
  And see, with every waif I burn,
Old dreams and fancies coloring it,
  And folly's unlaid ghosts return.

O ships of mine, whose swift keels cleft
  The enchanted sea on which they sailed,
Are these poor fragments only left
  Of vain desires and hopes that failed?

Did I not watch from them the light
  Of sunset on my towers in Spain,
And see, far off, uploom in sight
  The Fortunate Isles I might not gain?

Did sudden lift of fog reveal
  Arcadia's vales of song and spring,
And did I pass, with grazing keel,
  The rocks whereon the sirens sing?

Have I not drifted hard upon
  The unmapped regions lost to man,
The cloud-pitched tents of Prester John,
  The palace domes of Kubla Khan?

Did land winds blow from jasmine flowers,
  Where Youth the ageless Fountain fills?
Did Love make sign from rose blown bowers,
  And gold from Eldorado's hills?

Alas! the gallant ships, that sailed
  On blind Adventure's errand sent,
Howe'er they laid their courses, failed
  To reach the haven of Content.

And of my ventures, those alone
  Which Love had freighted, safely sped,
Seeking a good beyond my own,
  By clear-eyed Duty piloted.

O mariners, hoping still to meet
  The luck Arabian voyagers met,
And find in Bagdad's moonlit street
  Haroun al Raschid walking yet,

Take with you, on your Sea of Dreams,
  The fair, fond fancies dear to youth.
I turn from all that only seems,
  And seek the sober grounds of truth.

What matter that it is not May,
  That birds have flown, and trees are bare,
That darker grows the shortening day,
  And colder blows the wintry air!

The wrecks of passion and desire,
  The castles I no more rebuild,
May fitly feed my drift-wood fire,
  And warm the hands that age has chilled.

Whatever perished with my ships,
  I only know the best remains;
A song of praise is on my lips
  For losses which are now my gains.

Heap high my hearth! No worth is lost;
  No wisdom with the folly dies.
Burn on, poor shreds, your holocaust
  Shall be my evening sacrifice!

Far more than all I dared to dream,
  Unsought before my door I see;
On wings of fire and steeds of steam
  The world's great wonders come to me,

And holier signs, unmarked before,
  Of Love to seek and Power to save,—
The righting of the wronged and poor,
  The man evolving from the slave;

And life, no longer chance or fate,
  Safe in the gracious Fatherhood.
I fold o'er-wearied hands and wait,
  In full assurance of the good.

And well the waiting time must be,
  Though brief or long its granted days,
If Faith and Hope and Charity
  Sit by my evening hearth-fire's blaze.

And with them, friends whom Heaven has spared,
    Whose love my heart has comforted,
And, sharing all my joys, has shared
    My tender memories of the dead,—

Dear souls who left us lonely here,
    Bound on their last, long voyage, to whom
We, day by day, are drawing near,
    Where every bark has sailing room.

I know the solemn monotone
    Of waters calling unto me;
I know from whence the airs have blown
    That whisper of the Eternal Sea.

As low my fires of drift-wood burn,
    I hear that sea's deep sounds increase,
And, fair in sunset light, discern
    Its mirage-lifted Isles of Peace.

To Oliver Wendell Holmes

8th Mo. 29th, 1892.

Among the thousands who with hail and cheer
    Will welcome thy new year,
How few of all have passed, as thou and I,
    So many milestones by!

We have grown old together; we have seen,
    Our youth and age between,

Two generations leave us, and to-day
   We with the third hold way,

Loving and loved. If thought must backward run
   To those who, one by one,
In the great silence and the dark beyond
   Vanished with farewells fond,

Unseen not lost; our grateful memories still
   Their vacant places fill,
And, with the full-voiced greeting of new friends
   A tenderer whisper blends.

Linked close in a pathetic brotherhood
   Of mingled ill and good,
Of joy and grief, of grandeur and of shame,
   For pity more than blame,—

The gift is thine the weary world to make
   More cheerful for thy sake,
Soothing the ears its Miserere pains,
   With the old Hellenic strains,

Lighting the sullen face of discontent
   With smiles for blessings sent.
Enough of selfish wailing has been had,
   Thank God! for notes more glad.

Life is indeed no holiday; therein
   Are want, and woe, and sin,

Death and its nameless fears, and over all
   Our pitying tears must fall.

Sorrow is real; but the counterfeit
   Which folly brings to it,
We need thy wit and wisdom to resist,
   O rarest Optimist!

Thy hand, old friend! the service of our days,
   In differing moods and ways,
May prove to those who follow in our train
   Not valueless nor vain.

Far off, and faint as echoes of a dream,
   The songs of boyhood seem,
Yet on our autumn boughs, unflown with spring,
   The evening thrushes sing.

The hour draws near, howe'er delayed and late,
   When at the Eternal Gate
We leave the words and works we call our own,
   And lift void hands alone

For love to fill. Our nakedness of soul
   Brings to that Gate no toll;
Giftless we come to Him, who all things gives,
   And live because He lives.

BIOGRAPHICAL NOTE

John Greenleaf Whittier was born on December 17, 1807. Raised in a devout Quaker household, he had little formal schooling. He attended Haverhill Academy (1827–28) and supported himself as a shoemaker and a schoolteacher. He edited *American Manufacturer* in Boston (1829) and *Essex Gazette* (1830) in Haverhill before becoming editor of the important *New England Weekly Review* (1830–32). He published *Legends of New England in Prose and Verse* in 1831 and *Moll Pitcher* in 1832. He was a delegate to the national Republican party's 1831 convention and ran unsuccessfully for Congress the following year. Deeply involved in the anti-slavery movement, he urged immediate abolition in *Justice and Expediency* (1833). Elected to the Massachusetts legislature in 1834, Whittier served one term as a Whig. In 1836 he moved to Amesbury, New Hampshire. While he was editor of the *Pennsylvania Freeman* (1838–40), the paper's offices were burned and sacked by a mob. His collection *Poems* was published in 1838. Parting ways with abolitionist William Lloyd Garrison's radical tactics, Whittier founded the Liberty party in 1840 and ran unsuccessfully for Congress as its candidate in 1842. His abolitionist verse was gathered in *Voices of Freedom* (1846); a collected edition, *Poems by John G. Whittier*, appeared in 1849. His novel about 17th-century Massachusetts, *Leaves from Margaret Smith's Journal*, was published in 1849. He worked for the formation of the Republican party and supported the 1856 presidential bid of its candidate, John C. Frémont. His *Poetical Works* was published in 1857; the same year Whittier helped found the *Atlantic Monthly*. His close relationship with old friend Elizabeth Lloyd Howell led to consideration of marriage, but in 1859 he decided against it. His "winter idyl" *Snow-Bound* (1866) was his most popular work. From 1876 he lived most of the time with cousins in Danvers, Massachusetts, while retaining legal residence in Amesbury. The seven-volume Riverside Edition of his works, *The Writings of John Greenleaf Whittier*, was published in 1888–89. He died at Hampton Falls, New Hampshire, on September 7, 1892.

NOTE ON THE TEXTS

The poems in this volume are arranged in the approximate order of their composition, based on the chronological list included in the 1894 Cambridge Edition of Whittier's *Complete Poetical Works*. In general, the texts printed here are those of the poems' first publication in book form. The following list gives the date of each poem's composition (in parenthesis after the title) and indicates the source of the text as it is printed in this volume:

Toussaint l'Ouverture (1833): *Poems Written During the Progress of the Abolition Question* (Boston: Isaac Knapp, 1837).

The Demon of the Study (1835): *Lays of My Home, and Other Poems* (Boston: Williams D. Ticknor, 1843).

The Hunters of Men (1835): *Poems Written During the Progress of the Abolition Question* (Boston: Isaac Knapp, 1837).

The Farewell (1838): *Poems* (Philadelphia: J. Healy, 1838).

Massachusetts to Virginia (1843): *Lays of My Home, and Other Poems* (Boston: Williams D. Ticknor, 1843).

Song of Slaves in the Desert (1847): *The Panorama, and Other Poems* (Boston: Ticknor & Fields, 1856).

The Huskers (1847): *Songs of Labor, and Other Poems* (Boston: Ticknor, Reed, & Fields, 1850).

Proem (1847–49): *Poems* (Boston: B.B. Mussey & Co., 1849).

Lines on the Portrait of a Celebrated Publisher (1850): S. T. Pickard, *Life and Letters of John Greenleaf Whittier* (Boston: Houghton, Mifflin, 1894).

Ichabod! (1850): *Songs of Labor, and Other Poems* (Boston: Ticknor, Reed, & Fields, 1850).

A Sabbath Scene (1850): *The Chapel of the Hermits, and Other Poems* (Boston: Ticknor, Reed, & Fields, 1853).

The Haschish (1854): *The Panorama, and Other Poems* (Boston: Ticknor & Fields, 1856).

Moloch in State Street (1851): *Poetical Works* (Boston: Ticknor & Fields, 1857).

First-Day Thoughts (1852): *The Chapel of the Hermits, and Other Poems* (Boston: Ticknor, Reed, & Fields, 1853).

The Kansas Emigrants (1854): *The Panorama, and Other Poems* (Boston: Ticknor & Fields, 1856).

Maud Muller (1854): *The Panorama, and Other Poems* (Boston: Ticknor & Fields, 1856).

The Fruit-Gift (1854): *The Panorama, and Other Poems* (Boston: Ticknor & Fields, 1856).

The Barefoot Boy (1855): *The Panorama, and Other Poems* (Boston: Ticknor & Fields, 1856).

Letter (1855): *Anti-Slavery Poems: Songs of Labor and Reform* (Cambridge, MA: Riverside Press, 1888). Volume 3 of the Riverside Edition.

Skipper Ireson's Ride (1857): *Home Ballads and Poems* (Boston: Ticknor & Fields, 1860).

The Last Walk in Autumn (1857): *Poetical Works* (Boston: Ticknor & Fields, 1857).

The Garrison of Cape Ann (1857): *Home Ballads and Poems* (Boston: Ticknor & Fields, 1860).

Telling the Bees (1858): *Home Ballads and Poems* (Boston: Ticknor & Fields, 1860).

My Playmate (1860): *Home Ballads and Poems* (Boston: Ticknor & Fields, 1860).

The River Path (1860): James Head (ed.), *Jewels from the Quarry of the Mind* (Boston: Crosby, 1862).

"Ein feste Burg ist unser Gott" (1861): Frank Moore (ed.), *The Rebellion Record: A Diary of American Events*. First Volume (New York: Putnam, 1861).

The Waiting (1862): *In War Time and Other Poems* (Boston: Ticknor & Fields, 1868).

Barbara Frietchie (1863): *In War Time and Other Poems* (Boston: Ticknor & Fields, 1868).

The Vanishers (1864): *The Tent on the Beach and Other Poems* (Boston: Ticknor & Fields, 1867).

What the Birds Said (1864): *The Tent on the Beach and Other Poems* (Boston: Ticknor & Fields, 1867).

Laus Deo (1865): *National Lyrics* (Boston: Ticknor & Fields, 1865).

The Eternal Goodness (1865): *The Tent on the Beach and Other Poems* (Boston: Ticknor & Fields, 1867).

Snow-Bound (1866): *Snow-Bound: A Winter Idyl* (Boston: Ticknor & Fields, 1866).

from The Tent on the Beach (1866): *The Tent on the Beach and Other Poems* (Boston: Ticknor & Fields, 1867).

from Among the Hills: Prelude (1867): *Among the Hills and Other Poems* (Boston: Fields, Osgood & Co., 1869).

The Hive at Gettysburg (1868): *Miriam and Other Poems* (Boston: Fields, Osgood & Co., 1871).

In School-Days (1870): *Miriam and Other Poems* (Boston: Fields, Osgood & Co., 1871).

The Brewing of Soma (1872): *The Pennsylvania Pilgrim, and Other Poems* (Boston: Osgood, 1872).

The Pressed Gentian (1872): *The Vision of Echard and Other Poems* (Boston : Houghton, Osgood and Co., 1878).

The Witch of Wenham (1877): *The Vision of Echard and Other Poems* (Boston : Houghton, Osgood and Co., 1878).

The Henchman (1877): *The Vision of Echard and Other Poems* (Boston : Houghton, Osgood and Co., 1878).

At Last (1882): *The Bay of Seven Islands, and Other Poems* (Boston: Houghton, Mifflin, 1883).

Sweet Fern (1884): *Saint Gregory's Guest and Recent Poems* (Boston: Houghton, Mifflin, 1886).

Burning Drift-Wood (1890): *At Sundown* (Boston: Houghton, Mifflin, 1892).

To Oliver Wendell Holmes (1892): *At Sundown* (Boston: Houghton, Mifflin, 1892).

This volume presents the texts of the original printings chosen for inclusion here, but it does not attempt to reproduce nontextual features of their typographic design. The texts are presented without change, except for the correction of the following typographical errors, cited by page and line number: 1.12, crecopia; 3.28, Trode; 12.2, look; 13.2, chains; 14.2, our mountain; 20.21 father's; 60.26, Cannan; 71.9, Menu's; 73.16, colonade; 151.8, Wehnham.

NOTES

1.1   Toussaint l'Ouverture] "TOUSSAINT L'OUVERTURE, the black chieftain of Hayti, was a slave on the plantation of M. Bayon de Libertas. When the general rising of the negroes took place, in 1791, Toussaint refused to join them, until he had aided M. Bayon and his family to escape to Baltimore. The white man had discovered in Toussaint many noble qualities, and had instructed him in some of the first branches of education; and the preservation of his life is owing to the negro's gratitude for this kindness.

"In 1797, Toussaint L'Ouverture was appointed, by the French Government, General-in-Chief of the armies of St. Domingo, and as such, signed the Convention with General Maitland, for the evacuation of the island by the British. From this period until 1801, the island, under the government of Toussaint, was happy, tranquil, and prosperous. The miserable attempt by Napoleon to re-establish slavery in St. Domingo, although it failed of its intended object, proved fatal to the Negro chieftain. Treacherously seized by Leclerc, he was hurried on board a vessel by night, and conveyed to France, where he was confined in a cold subterranean dungeon, at Besancon, where, in April, 1803, he died. The treatment of Toussaint finds a parallel only in the murder of the Duke d'Enghein. It was the remark of Godwin, in his Lectures, that the West Indian islands, since their discovery by Columbus, could not boast of a single name which deserved comparison with that of TOUSSAINT L'OUVERTURE." (Whittier's note.)

8.16   dungeon-tomb] "The reader may, perhaps, call to mind the beautiful sonnet of William Wordsworth, addressed to Toussaint L'Ouverture, during his confinement in France.

> 'Toussaint!—thou most unhappy man of men!
>   Whether the whistling rustic tend his plough
>   Within thy hearing, or thou liest now
> Buried in some deep dungeon's earless den;—
> Oh, miserable chieftain!— where and when
>   Wilt thou find patience?—Yet, die not; do thou
>   Wear rather in thy bonds a cheerful brow:
> Though fallen thyself never to rise again,
> Live and take comfort. Thou hast left behind
>   Powers that will work for thee; air, earth, and skies,—
> There's not a breathing of the common wind
>   That will forget thee: thou hast great allies.
> Thy friends are exultations, agonies,
>   And love, and man's unconquerable mind.'" (Whittier's note.)

9.21   The Demon . . . Study] "From unpublished 'Papers of a Quiet Man.'" (Whittier's note.)

10.1   shade of Denmark] Hamlet's father.

10.2   Cocklane ghost] In 1762, William Parsons of London claimed that the ghost of recently deceased Fanny Kent was making mysterious noises in his home. In the hopes of blackmailing Kent's husband, Parsons sought to convince people that Fanny had been murdered. Parsons' home in Cock Lane attracted numerous curious visitors until it was revealed that the noises were made by his 11-year-old daughter.

12.23   Hylas] In Greek mythology, a boy abducted by water nymphs who were enchanted by his beauty. He was Hercules' beloved.

13.4   Glanville] English theologian Joseph Glanvill (1636–1680), author of *Witches and Witchcraft* (1666), who defended belief in the occult.

13.10   Brady and Tate] Nahum Brady and Nicholas Tate's metrical "New Version" of the Psalms (1696).

13.16–17   *Conjuro . . . locum*] I command you, most evil one, to go back where you came from.

21.24   'cleaving curse'] A phrase from Milton's "Of Reformation in England" (1641). Cf. Whittier's "The Republican Party" (1885): "Then may the language which Milton addressed to his countrymen two centuries ago be applied to the United States, 'Go on, hand in hand, O peoples, never to be disunited; be the praise and heroic song of all posterity. Join your invincible might to do worthy and godlike deeds; and then he who seeks to break your Union, a cleaving curse be his inheritance.'"

23.21   Latimer!] The escaped slave George Latimer was arrested in Boston in November 1842 in an attempt by Virginia planter James Gray to claim him under the terms of the 1793 federal Fugitive Slave Law. A court ruling placed Latimer in the custody of Gray, who was given ten days to provide evidence of his claim. Ordered to remain in Massachusetts until a hearing on the case, Gray paid the county jailer to detain Latimer, causing widespread public outrage. Judge Lemuel Shaw then ruled that state courts could not interfere with fugitive slave cases pending in federal court. Petitions were circulated calling for a law prohibiting state officials to assist in the capture and incarceration of fugitive slaves (a law that was passed the following year). On November 15, Latimer was released from detention. Gray acknowledged Latimer's freedom in exchange for Latimer's promise not to sue him for false imprisonment and the payment of a sum raised by local abolitionists.

25.6   Song . . . Desert] The poem was suggested by the following passage in the African journal of the English abolitionist James Richardson (1806–1851), as quoted by Whittier in the 1888 Riverside Edition: "*Sebah, Oasis of Fezzan, 10th March, 1846.*—This evening the female slaves were unusually excited in singing, and I had the curiosity to ask my negro servant, Said, what they were singing about. As many of them were natives of his own country, he had no difficulty in translating the Mandara or Bornou language. I had often asked the Moors to translate their songs for me, but got no satisfactory account from them. Said at first said, 'Oh, they sing of Rubee' (God). 'What do you mean?' I replied, impatiently. 'Oh, don't you know?' he continued, 'they asked God to give them their Atka?' (certificate of freedom). I inquired, 'Is that all?' Said: 'No; they say, "Where are we going? The world is large. O God! Where are we going? O God!"' I inquired, 'What else?' Said: 'They remember their country, Bornou, and say, "Bornou was a pleasant country, full of all good things; but this is a bad country, and we are miserable!"' 'Do they say anything else?' Said: 'No; they repeat these words over and over again, and add, "O God! give us our Atka, and let us return again to our dear home."'" Bornou is a region of West Africa, mostly in what is now northeastern Nigeria.

25.19   Dourra]   Indian millet, common grain in parts of Africa.

34.4   Celebrated Publisher]   Louis Godey (1804–1878), who had refused to publish the writings of Grace Greenwood (the pseudonym of Sarah Jane Clarke) in his popular magazine *Godey's Lady's Book* because of her abolitionist views.

36.9   Ichabod!]   Hebrew: "inglorious"; a child (1 Samuel 4:21) so named by his mother who died giving him birth. Whittier applies the epithet to Daniel Webster for his support of the Compromise of 1850, which included the passage of a new Fugitive Slave Law.

43.8   Shitan]   Form of Arabic Shaitan, "Satan-like."

43.22   raving Cuban filibuster!]   Pro-slavery expansionists advocated the annexation of Cuba in the years before the Civil War, and had supported two filibustering expeditions in 1850–51.

44.8   Gentoo]   Hindu.

45.14–15   Moloch's fire . . . flesh]   Some scriptural interpretations have suggested that children were sacrificed to the Phoenician god Molech (Moloch). See Leviticus 18:21: "And thou shalt not let any of thy seed pass through the fire to Molech."

47.8   name]   "The election of Charles Sumner to the U.S. Senate 'followed hard upon' the rendition of the fugitive Sims by the U.S. officials and the armed police of Boston." (Whittier's note.) Thomas Sims, an escaped slave from Georgia, was arrested in Boston on April 3, 1851, and kept in the courthouse under heavy guard until April 12, when he was escorted to the harbor by 300 armed deputies and militiamen and placed on a ship bound for Savannah, Georgia. Efforts to buy his freedom were unsuccessful, and Sims was sold at auction.

47.14   First-Day]   Quaker term for Sunday.

55.11   the Prophet's]   Amos (see Amos 8:1).

55.17–18   homeward-turning Jew . . . clusters]   See Numbers 13:23–24, in which the men sent by Moses to "spy out the land of Canaan" cut down a cluster of grapes by the brook of Eshcol and return with the fruit as evidence of the land's abundance.

58.15   Apples of Hesperides!]   Golden apples given to Hera as a wedding present.

61.3   the Nebraska bill]   The Kansas-Nebraska Act, signed into law in 1854, established Kansas and Nebraska as federal territories. The law repealed the prohibition against slavery in federal territory north of 36° 30′ and allowed the question of whether slavery would be permitted in the new territories to be decided by their elected legislatures.

61.27   wild beasts of Ephesus]   See 1 Corinthians 15:32.

61.28   Long John]   "Long John" Wentworth (1815–1888), lawyer, abolitionist journalist and congressman.

62.19–27   far bayous . . . Quitman's bowie-knife]   John Anthony Quitman (1798–1858), governor of Mississippi, had recruited soldiers and procured arms for an 1850 filibustering expedition to Cuba (see note 43.22). For his involvement in the mission he was indicted for violating federal neutrality laws but was acquitted in court. He organized another expedition and by the spring of 1854 had recruited thousands of volunteers. These soldiers assembled in Louisiana, awaiting orders for the invasion force to embark. Despite substantial backing by Southern politicians, efforts to suspend the neutrality laws were thwarted when the Pierce administration withdrew its support, and Quitman's expedition was canceled.

63.5   Calendar's horse of brass]   Featured in "The Tale of the Third Kalandar" in *The Arabian Nights*.

63.7   Al-Borák]   White winged animal, somewhere between a donkey and a mule in height, on which Muhammad is said to have made a journey to the seven heavens.

63.10   Floyd Ireson]   "In the valuable and carefully prepared History of Marblehead, published in 1879 by Samuel Roads, Jr., it is stated that the crew of Captain Ireson, rather than himself, were responsible for the abandonment of the disabled vessel. To screen themselves they charged their captain with the crime." (From Whittier's note in the 1888 Riverside Edition.)

69.12   Pharpar's]   One of the two "rivers of Damascus" alluded to in 2 Kings 5:12.

82.20   Telling the Bees]   "A remarkable custom, brought from the Old Country, formerly prevailed in the rural districts of New England. On the death of a member of the family, the bees were at once informed of the event, and their hives dressed in mourning. This ceremonial was supposed to be necessary to prevent the swarms from leaving their hives and seeking a new home." (Whittier's note.)

90.1   "Ein . . . Gott"]   A mighty fortress is our God: the first line of a hymn written by Martin Luther. The poem follows the meter of the hymn.

94.6   Barbara Frietchie]   "It is admitted by all that Barbara Frietchie was no myth, but a worthy and highly esteemed gentlewoman, intensely loyal and a hater of the Slavery Rebellion, holding her Union flag sacred and keeping it with her Bible; that when the Confederates halted before her house, and entered her dooryard, she denounced them in vigorous language, shook her cane in their faces, and drove them out; and when General Burnside's troops followed close upon Jackson's, she waved her flag and cheered them. It is stated that May Quantrell, a brave and loyal lady in another part of the city, did wave her flag in sight of the Confederates. It is possible that there has been a blending of the two incidents." (From Whittier's note in the 1888 Riverside Edition.)

110.25   Amun]   Ram-headed Egyptian deity.

115.1   "The Chief . . . shore."]   A line from Sarah Wentworth Morton's "The African Chief," poem collected in Caleb Bingham's *The American Preceptor* (the "school-book" to which Whittier refers at 114.30).

115.5   Dame Mercy Warren's]   Writer (1728–1814) and activist in the American Revolution.

116.13–14   Indian hordes . . . Cochecho town]   Dover, on the Cocheco River in New Hampshire, was attacked by Indians on June 28, 1689.

116.25   wizard's conjuring-book]   "I have in my possession the wizard's 'conjuring book' . . . It is a copy of Cornelius Agrippa's Magic, printed in 1651." (From Whittier's note in the 1888 Riverside Edition.)

117.10   Sewell's ancient tome]   *The History, Rise, Increase and Progress of the Christian People Called Quakers* (London, 1722) by William Sewell (1654–1720).

117.13   Chalkley's Journal]   The often reprinted *Journal* (1766) of the itinerant Quaker preacher Thomas Chalkley (1675–1741).

118.26   White of Selborne's]   Gilbert White (1720–1793), English naturalist, author of *The Natural History and Antiquities of Selborne* (1789).

124.23   Another guest]   Harriet Livermore (1788–1867), described by Whittier in the 1888 Riverside Edition as "a young woman of fine natural ability, enthusiastic, eccentric, with slight control over her violent temper, which sometimes made her religious profession doubtful. . . . She early embraced the doctrine of the Second Advent, and felt it her duty to proclaim the Lord's speedy coming. With this message she crossed the Atlantic and spent the greater part of a long life in travelling over Europe and Asia."

126.8   Queen of Lebanon]   Lady Hester Lucy Stanhope (1776–1839), who established a fortified estate at Mt. Lebanon in 1814 and, adopting Eastern dress, proclaimed a religion that combined Christian and Islamic beliefs. She engaged in intrigues against the British consuls in the district and exercised almost despotic power over the tribal people in the area, who considered her a prophet.

130.15–18   Ellwood's . . . Jews]   Thomas Ellwood (1639–1713), Quaker poet and pamphleteer, author of *Davideis: The Life of King David in Israel, a Sacred Poem* (1712).

130.26   McGregor]   Sir Gregory McGregor, Scottish adventurer who arrived in Caracas in 1817 and fought under Bolivar; later he made numerous raids around the Caribbean before settling on the Mosquito Coast of Central America and calling himself His Highness, the Cacique of Pogair.

130.29   Ypsilanti's Mainote Greeks]   Demetrius Ypsilanti (1793–1832), Greek patriot and commander, successfully defended Argos in a key battle with the Turks.

140.22   knife-grinder . . . Canning]   George Canning (1770–1827), English statesman and poet, wrote "The Friend of Humanity and the Knife-Grinder."

142.10–17   the old Hebrew myth . . . strong heart.]   See Judges 14:8, in which the young Samson, on his way to see a woman he would soon marry, came upon the carcass of a lion he had killed with his bare hands. The animal's corpse was swarming with bees and filled with honey. At his wedding feast he posed the riddle, "Out of the eater came forth meat, and out of the strong came forth sweetness."

165.20   Prester John]   Imaginary Christian emperor purported to rule a kingdom in Asia.

INDEX OF TITLES
AND FIRST LINES

AMERICAN POETS PROJECT

EDNA ST. VINCENT MILLAY: SELECTED POEMS
J. D. McClatchy, editor
ISBN 1-931082-35-9

POETS OF WORLD WAR II
Harvey Shapiro, editor
ISBN 1-931082-33-2

KARL SHAPIRO: SELECTED POEMS
John Updike, editor
ISBN 1-931082-34-0

WALT WHITMAN: SELECTED POEMS
Harold Bloom, editor
ISBN 1-931082-32-4

EDGAR ALLAN POE: POEMS AND POETICS
Richard Wilbur, editor
ISBN 1-931082-51-0

YVOR WINTERS: SELECTED POEMS
Thom Gunn, editor
ISBN 1-931082-50-2

AMERICAN WITS: AN ANTHOLOGY OF LIGHT VERSE
John Hollander, editor
ISBN 1-931082-49-9

KENNETH FEARING: SELECTED POEMS
Robert Polito, editor
ISBN 1-931082-57-x

MURIEL RUKEYSER: SELECTED POEMS
Adrienne Rich, editor
ISBN 1-931082-58-8

JOHN GREENLEAF WHITTIER
Brenda Wineapple, editor
ISBN 1-931082-59-6